My Darkest Days, My Brightest Future

Allison Craig

NEWMAN SPRINGS PUBLISHING
320 Broad Street
Red Bank, NJ 07701

First originally published by Newman Springs Publishing 2019

ISBN 978-1-64531-782-1 (Paperback)
ISBN 978-1-64531-783-8 (Digital)

Printed in the United States of America

To Brendan
For always believing in me, supporting me, and encouraging
me. You never judged me because of my mistakes.

To Norm
For picking up the pieces, loving me, and treating
me the way a man should treat a woman.

The true story of one woman's twenty-year struggle and determination to hold together an impossible relationship and the eventual realization of her lifelong dream.

Acknowledgments

NUMEROUS FAMILY AND FRIENDS SUPPORTED me during those difficult twenty years in ways not related to the actual writing of this book, but to holding myself together and persevering. Some of you may not even realize how you helped me. There are too many to name.

As far as writing this book, I am a voracious reader, and I received invaluable help from the following authors: Dan Pink and Carmine Gallo; Darren Hardy, author, public speaker, and personal development guru. Your Darren Dailies motivated me to keep writing on a consistent basis when I had taken a long hiatus from writing. I cannot forget my core Toastmasters group, Victoria, Donna, Garey, Barb, and John, who, sadly, is no longer with us. Our group inspired me, instructed me, and coached me on how to put together and deliver a speech. Those lessons contributed to helping me write this book. My dear friend, Susan, who at the last minute provided me with priceless insights.

Introduction

"How much of each relationship is based on reality versus what we hope to believe about who the other is?" (Maggie Walther). While Maggie Walther is a fictional character in Richard Paul Evans' lovely book, *The Noel Stranger*, I am a real person, and not a work of fiction. How I wished I would have asked myself this question, among others, many years ago.

How do you determine if you should stay in a relationship with someone? How can you live with someone for years and not be able to decide? How can you put up with very serious issues and still stay in the relationship? How can anyone who hears your story not think you are out of your mind to stay in a relationship that is not good for you in so many ways? How many times do you forgive someone and just let it go? How do you determine if there is more good in a person than bad? How do you determine if someone has mental issues and really cannot help what they do? How do you determine if someone is without feelings for anyone but themselves? How do you know if you have done enough to keep the relationship going, or if there is more you can do but you just don't know what the "more" is? How many years do you have to know someone before you can say you really know them? How do you determine if your relationship is a facade?

These are the questions I spent years trying to answer by seeking medical advice, reading articles and books, and praying my heart out because I wanted to do the right thing, because I did not want another failed marriage, because I had many regrets from my first marriage and didn't want any from this one.

PART 1

Maryland

CHAPTER 1

Growing Up

I AM AN ONLY CHILD. My mother was born and raised in Baltimore City with her parents and six siblings. She was the only one of her siblings to graduate from high school and have a church wedding. My mom wanted to be a doctor, and she was smart enough to be one, but because of the financial circumstances within her family, she got a job right out of high school and contributed to the family's needs. She always told me her family was poor but so happy they didn't know they were poor. Mom loved butterflies, ladybugs, the color blue, and especially Christmas. One year, she left our real Christmas tree up until Easter!

It wasn't until after Mom died, while visiting my aunt, I found out her childhood was not the happy time she made it out to be. I don't believe Mom deliberately lied about her childhood, but saying it was happy was the only way she could deal with it. My grandparents argued constantly. Mom used to sit on her bed and cover her ears with her hands to try and block out my grandparents' yelling at each other. The only time they did not argue was Christmas day. That explained why my Mom loved Christmas so much. I think Mom may have suffered from depression but was never diagnosed or treated.

Mom was a quiet, gentle person. Everyone loved her. She never punished me but would explain to me what I had done wrong and why it was wrong. Mom did not yell at me or hit me. She treated me with great respect and, most times, left it up to me to make my own decisions so I could have experience and learn for myself from those experiences. For example, I never had a bedtime even when I was in grade school. She said if I was dumb enough to stay up late, I would be tired the next day for school. I stayed up late one of my first nights in grade school. The next day, I was so sleepy I could hardly keep my eyes open. After that, I made sure I went to bed early on school nights to get a good night's sleep. I think I was the only person in my high school who did not have a curfew. I had to tell Mom where I was going and what time I would be home. If my plans changed, and I was going to be out later, I had to call and let her know. She trusted me completely, and I think that was why I did not do drugs or get into trouble at school. I did not want to hurt or upset Mom. All my friends loved my mom and told me they wished she was their mom. They confided in her and would tell her things they would never tell their parents.

My father was born in Canton, Ohio. When he was six years old, his family moved back to Spain where his parents were from originally. He had two sisters, and the one he was closest to died in her early thirties. My father never got over her loss. There was a civil war raging in Spain during Pop's childhood, and when he was old enough, he became a bullfighter to help with the family finances. He killed 102 bulls and was never gored. After his bullfighting career, he joined the Foreign Legion and was stationed in North Africa. The Foreign Legion was tough; there was no retreat, and after one battle, only he and eight other men returned. On a march across the desert, one of the men complained his feet hurt. The commanding officer shot the soldier dead and then asked if anyone else's feet hurt.

In his early twenties, Pop emigrated to the United States. I never met his parents because they stayed in Spain. Pop's goal was to earn enough money to send for his fiancé and bring her and her father to the United States. Unfortunately, a few weeks after he left Spain, she took up with another man, so my father decided to stay in America. Pop shared an apartment with a friend who was the boyfriend of my aunt. One year, on Thanksgiving, Pop's friend invited him to Thanksgiving dinner at my aunt's, and that was how my parents met.

Mom had been engaged to another man, but he was killed in the war. By the time my parents met, they had both been hurt romantically and, at this point, were older. Mom was thirty-five and Pop was thirty-two when they married. Since my parents did not have a happy marriage, I often wondered if they married out of convenience or because they could not have the person they really wanted to marry. I have a photo of them on their honeymoon at Niagara Falls, and it is the only time I ever saw them holding hands. By the time I was born, Mom was forty years old.

We lived in a large three-story Victorian house with my mom's parents and two of her sisters, their husbands, and children. When I was three years old, Mom sold all our furniture and left my father. She took me to California, and we lived with one of her sisters. Even though I was little, I remember being sick the entire three days we were on the bus to California. One of my cousins we lived with teased me and tormented me constantly, so the time we lived in California was not a happy time for me. My father had sent me a picture of him outside the door of his office, and I looked at it all the time and cried for him. I still have the picture. For whatever reason(s), after two years in California, Mom and I moved back to Maryland, and Mom reconciled with my father.

My mother's mom moved in with us, and while she and my father never argued, they did not get along. Mom was always in the middle of the two of them. She said she was always standing between two fires. My father worked swing shift, and when he was on nights, my grandmother had the TV up loud, so Pop couldn't sleep, and that made matters even worse. This put more of a strain on my parent's already fragile marriage. Eventually, my grandmother went to live with one of her other children.

I never knew what the problems were in my parent's marriage, only that my parents were not like my friends' parents; they never went out together and left me with a sitter, and I never saw them display any sort of physical affection toward one another. As I got older, my parents made it known to me they were not happily married, and each would tell tales to me about the other one behind each other's back. I didn't like hearing these things because I did not want to take sides, and there was nothing I could do about the situation. However, I believe they both did the best they could under the circumstances. Despite my parents' differences, I feel I had a good and happy childhood. Just before my mom passed away, my parents did express their love for one another.

Our home was modest. We never had much money, but we were not poor. My mom was an exceptional seamstress, and whenever I needed an outfit for a special occasion (dance at school, special date, etc.), she would make something for me that was the envy of everyone else. She made a lot of my everyday clothes, and friends of mine always wanted to borrow my patterns to copy what my mom had made for me. Mom continued making special occasion clothes for me, even after I had married. When it was time for me to attend school, Mom went back to work full time so I could attend a parochial school. She felt it was important I receive a religious education.

Growing up, I absolutely loved school. I got decent grades, my teachers were wonderful, I had lots of friends, always had a boyfriend, and was a cheerleader in high school. I went to many school activities and dances. I dated only one guy at a time. When I was fourteen years old, I met my first boyfriend, and we were together for three years. Next, I dated a guy in my high school for several years, and we even got engaged, but that did not work out, and I broke off the engagement.

I received a college preparatory education, but going to college was a different story. I hated it, I think, because all my academic life, I had attended very small schools, and the college I attended was a large university. I felt lost. I also did not have a clue what I wanted to major in. Because I had always loved going to school, I thought I might become a schoolteacher; maybe even return to my high school to teach. Truthfully, all I really wanted was to get married and have my own home, be a wife and a mom not because I wanted to get away from my parents but because that was simply what I wanted to do. At the time, I felt embarrassed and ashamed about what I wanted to do with my life. It did not seem to be an important goal. Women were encouraged to get a degree, have a meaningful career.

Reflecting to that time, I realize now I should not have felt the way I did. This was my dream—how I wanted my life to turn out. It was simple but not meaningless or unimportant. Not everyone has the resources of Bill and Melinda Gates. Mother Teresa said, "Not all of us can do great things, but we can do small things with great love." If I was happy and well-adjusted, the people around me—my family, friends, neighbors and acquaintances—would benefit.

As a result of my feelings and lack of interest in college, I quit college four days into my second year. I also did not want my parents spending money that they didn't have if I was not going to do anything with a college education. It was then a high school friend of mine told me about a job selling furniture at the furniture store where she worked. I interviewed and was hired even though I had no experience selling furniture. That was where I met Brendan's dad. After four years of dating, when I was twenty-three years old, we married.

CHAPTER 2

Meeting Peter

I FIRST MET PETER WHEN I was in the process of leaving my husband. On the surface, it seemed my first marriage was a very successful one. We had everything—a large custom-built house on over two acres, good jobs, nice cars, an expensive vacation every year to Walt Disney World, and a beautiful healthy three-year-old boy. However, things were not good between us, and eighteen years later, the marriage ended in divorce.

I was able to purchase a beautiful four-story townhouse in an upscale neighborhood just ten minutes from the house my ex-husband and I lived in, which made it convenient for us to have joint custody of Brendan. Brendan would spend four days with me and then go to his dad's house for four days.

My plan was to get a divorce, get settled and, hopefully, to marry again. At the time, I had a very good job working in a large and prestigious general surgery practice where I oversaw the billing department and computer system. The computer tech, who had serviced our computers for seven years, was fired, and Peter was his replacement. Peter blew into my life like a tornado, and from the day I met him, he pursued me relentlessly despite the fact he was twenty-seven years old, and I was forty at the time. Even though it was not in my plans to enter a relationship at the time, I fell for him.

Peter seemed to be a breath of fresh air and not what I was used to. He was spontaneous, to say the least, where I had always been a by-the-book girl, cautious, and conservative. What really won me over was how he treated my son, Brendan. I was not looking forward to being a single parent, and I desperately wanted a stable two-parent home for my son. Peter was outgoing, friendly, warm to everyone, and he treated Brendan like his own immediately. Brendan loved being around Peter simply because Peter was fun to be with. In spite of how I was raised and my religious beliefs, I let Peter move in with me and kept it a secret from Brendan. At Brendan's young age, it was easy to hide the fact Peter was living with me.

After knowing me a short time, Peter asked me to marry him. My divorce was not even final, and I felt he should find someone closer to his own age. His response was that he found women his age immature and wanted an older woman, and as far as Brendan was concerned, he wanted a "microwave" (instant) family. He always seemed to say just the right thing. I still had the divorce to go through, a son and, eventually, an ex-husband (baggage). When I was thirty-one, I had breast cancer, which resulted in a double mas-tectomy with reconstruction—in other words, a chest that was not very appealing. None of this seemed to matter to Peter. He asked me every single day to marry him. Not two months after my divorce, on July 1, 1999, we were married in the county courthouse. I did love him, but the guilt of living together without being married was what caused me to marry him before I felt I was ready. Even if I had waited longer, I know I would have married him anyway.

CHAPTER 3

Warning Signs and Illusions

THERE WERE SOME THINGS ABOUT Peter that bothered me from the start. Once we began seeing one another, he told me had spent two years in prison (not jail) for armed robbery when he was in his early twenties. His explanation was he hung around with the wrong people in college, and it was a stupid, spontaneous thing he did. Even though I had only known him for a short time at this point, I could hardly believe he had done such a thing. However, people do make mistakes, and he had served his time, so I felt he deserved a second chance. There are plenty of people who break the law, serve out their sentence, and go on to lead law-abiding productive lives. I appreciated his honesty and candor about the situation.

Not long after we met, Peter said he was "like a chameleon"— he could fit right into any group/class of people or situation. When he said that, I almost got a cold chill, but I brushed it off and told myself he was a people person, and that was a good thing.

I caught Peter in several lies early on in our relationship. He told me he made $60,000.00 a year. I could not believe that. I knew the previous engineer for our office computer system rather well—where he lived, the car he drove, etc.—and it was not the lifestyle of someone making that kind of money, but I could not prove otherwise. Before we married, Peter always seemed to have a lot of money to spend. I found out later that was because he did not have car insurance (in Maryland, it is against the law not to), and the car he drove was a wreck his father had fixed up and given him. Peter moved to

Maryland not long after his release from prison after being hired for his current job with his clothes and, literally, a fork, spoon, and knife. After we married, I found out he made about $30,000.00 a year.

When I first met Peter, his company had a small satellite office in an office building near his apartment. I met him there one day after work, and before we left, I followed him down the hall to the janitor's closet where he proceeded to take rolls of toilet paper. I asked what he was doing, and he told me if the closet was unlocked, he helped himself. I had been raised to be brutally honest, and this disturbed me a great deal, but I chalked it up to his immigrant family and that they had to struggle, whereas while my family was not wealthy, we certainly were not so bad off we had to steal things.

Not long after we met, he gave me a gold butterfly pin and told me he had bought it in an antique store. On one of our trips back to visit his family, we stopped at a truck stop to use the restroom. I noticed pins exactly like the one he had given me in the display case at the truck stop. I chalked it up to him wanting to impress me.

Several days after Peter moved in with me, I overheard him on his cell phone. My townhouse was four stories with winding staircases, which meant that one could lean over the railing on the third level and look down all the way to the basement, sound easily carried. Peter was in the basement and I was walking past the staircase on the second level and I could not help but overhear his conversation. He was telling someone that I was old, we didn't have an active sex life (which was a lie), and he and I were not a good match. This infuriated me, and I immediately confronted him. I told him to take his things and leave. At this point, he only had a few things he had brought over, so it did not take him long to put everything in his car and leave. The next day, he called me and, somehow, was able to convince me to let him come back. How I wish I had trusted my instincts and not let him return.

Peter's driving was beyond atrocious to the point I felt unsafe in the car with him and, literally, held on whenever I rode with him. In the beginning of our relationship, I obviously didn't want to say anything to him or appear to be critical, but once I got to know him better, I did bring up the subject. He blew it off, but from then on, I drove most of the time we went anywhere together. Peter told me he loved to drive, and he seemed to derive pleasure from driving aggressively and unsafely. Not long after he moved to Maryland, he acquired four tickets in one day—three from speeding and one because he was not wearing his seat belt. I remember letting him take Brendan somewhere after we were married, and when they came home, Brendan told me he watched the speedometer reach 100 miles per hour! At the time, Brendan was around nine or ten years old, and he thought that was cool. I blew a gasket over that one and told Peter if he wanted to kill himself, that was fine, but not to take my son with him. I never let Brendan go in the car with Peter again.

A few months after we married, Peter and I took Brendan and Peter's niece and nephew to Walt Disney World. Even though we had three kids with us, it was sort of a honeymoon because we did not take one when we married. Peter insisted we take my wedding dress and his tux so we could have our picture taken in front of the castle. I reluctantly agreed. I felt like an idiot riding on the bus to the Magic Kingdom in a wedding dress, Peter in his tux, and both of us wearing wedding Mickey Mouse ears. We did have our picture taken in front of the castle right before a cast member informed us we had to change our clothes because guests were not allowed to walk around the park dressed like a princess. I didn't realize it at the time, but Peter was all about appearances; it didn't matter how things really were—all that mattered was how they appeared to be.

About two years after we married, Peter joined my church. He had been attending since we became a couple. He willingly did everything he was supposed to do—attended all the meetings, volunteered for church activities and projects, served members who were in need—all things that were seen by the members, but the things he was supposed to do behind closed doors he didn't consistently do and only when initiated by me. He never said his prayers; he told me he didn't feel worthy to speak to God. He never read or studied the Scriptures. Only occasionally did he and I pray together or read the Scriptures together.

One Christmas during the time we had our store, the three of us came home in the evening to find three large boxes wrapped as

Christmas gifts on our front porch. There was an anonymous card with them. Brendan's box had various toys he wanted, Peter's box had about thirty DVDs (none of which he already had), and my box had several Byer's Choice Carolers (none of which I already had). There had to be several hundred dollars' worth of gifts between the three of us. We had a few friends who had the means to do such a thing, and it was no secret we were struggling financially. I contacted our friends, but none of them would own up to leaving the gifts.

After Christmas, Peter began pulling money out of the large book collection I had in our loft. The bills were small, and any time we wanted to do something, that is, go bowling, see a movie, take a day trip to Washington, DC, he would pull cash out from between the pages of the books. I asked him where he got the money, but he wouldn't say.

You would think I was smart enough to put two and two together and figure all this out, but I think I didn't want to figure it out. I was determined this marriage was going to work. I used to run errands for my aunt, and she would always "tip" me even though I did not want to accept any money from her. I put the money aside, and it added up over time to around $800.00 in small bills. I kept the money in a secret drawer in our chest of drawers in our bedroom. Peter and Brendan knew about the money and where I kept it. Several months after Peter used up his hidden stash, I looked, and I had less than $200.00 in the secret drawer. I confronted Peter, and he said Brendan must have taken it. I knew Brendan would never do such a thing. I am sure Peter took that money to buy the "anonymous" Christmas gifts and to have the cash stuffed in my books to use on occasion. Peter always told me he would steal money from me before he would cheat on me.

On one of our trips to visit Peter's family, I met his childhood best friend and asked him if there was only one thing he could tell me about Peter, what would it be. He told me that Peter acts now and then thinks about what he has done later. I came to realize as time went by that was how Peter rolled. Many times, he never gave a second thought to the things he did.

These lies and fabrications of his should have been a huge red flag, but I guess, in retrospect, I didn't want to admit that to myself. The warning signs were numerous and constant, but I always made excuses for him and laid the blame on his bipolar disorder, his depression, his ADHD, his OCD, his addictive tendencies, the trauma he experienced growing up, etc. After reading and researching extensively on mental disorders, I realized Peter's brain was not wired the way most brains were wired. I used to joke with him that either he did not get a prefrontal cortex, or the one he had was broken because the prefrontal cortex is where one's impulse control is located. I always believed with the right combination of medication, the right therapist/psychiatrist, and my patience, love, and forgiveness, he would get better and stop doing the things he did. It would be years before I found out what was really going on with him.

CHAPTER 4

Peter's Family and Childhood

WHEN I BEGAN THIS BOOK, I asked Peter to tell me about his family and his childhood. These are his own words:

> I was born on January 23, 1970, in Ho Chi Minh City, better known as Saigon. My first memories are like Polaroid pictures; no sounds or movement in them. I don't remember my room or any toys I might have had. My first memory is of a barren field with barbed wire fences around it. I think it was a mine field. My next memory is being in line in a church, and there was popcorn around where Jesus was laid. The next memory was playing in our neighborhood. There was a well, and I used to put little chicks in a pail and let them ride down into the well and then back out. My dad's parent's house was huge, and I fell down the steps and got the wind knocked out of me. I remember being on a beach and ducking behind a piece of wood and hearing bullets on the other side of the wood. Next, I remember being on an oil tanker after being on a small fishing boat. There were two wooden planks off the side of the oil tanker, and that was the bathroom. You could look down and see the waves beneath

you. We were dropped off on Guam, but I have no memories of it. We were sponsored over to the States. I remember being in a glass room going up and down and up and down. It was an elevator in a Holiday Inn in Hawaii. Next, I was at Norfolk International Airport and remember seeing a dog in a carrier. I asked my mom how to say dog in English. That was my first English word.

I was five years old, my sister Mary was three years old, and my sister Ann was about ten weeks old. My next memory is being the little drummer boy in a Christmas play. I went into kindergarten not speaking any English. By the time I got to first grade, I was speaking English. I had an assignment in second or third grade to draw an animal. I drew a beautiful macaw bird and somebody at school said I didn't draw it and I got into a fight over it. My mom had to come to school to tell the teacher I did draw it. That was the first time I got into trouble at school. The next time was over a girl in second grade. I stole two pennies from another kid to give to the girl. The teacher had a paddle, and I got my hands slapped with the paddle as punishment. I got into trouble at school maybe once a year, but I did get into trouble at home frequently.

One time, my parents had gone out, and we were supposed to stay inside while they were gone. I went outside, and Mary locked me out. I was between ten and twelve years old. I broke the pane of glass in the back door to get in and cut my arm. I got into big trouble over breaking the glass. There was a weeping willow tree in our backyard, and I had to pick out the branch I was going to get whipped by. This was a frequent form of punishment at our house. We also

got beat with belts and cords. Both of my parents abused me and my siblings physically when
we had misbehaved. In addition to being beat
with the tree branch, my parents made me stand
naked on our front porch for two hours to shame
me in front of our neighbors.

Another time, when I was in my teens, I
broke into our garage to get tools to work on my
bike and skateboard. I had taken my father's tools
many times and not returned them, so he had
locked me out of the garage. On this occasion, I
found my father's collection of *Playboy* magazines,
looked through them, and did not put them back
the way my father had them. When my father
realized what I had done, I got a broomstick
handle broken across my behind and an exten-
sion cord used to whip me. My mother blamed
my father for the magazines and, subsequently,
burned all of them in a drum in our yard.

I was frequently a bad example for my siblings. I used to stand on the back bumper holding onto the cap of my dad's truck as he pulled
out of the long driveway, and just as he was leaving the driveway, at the end, I would step off.
One time, when my sister Mary was not at home,
but Sam and Ann were, I was in the front yard,
and Ann and Sam were on the back of the truck.
They were little at the time. Ann let go in the
driveway and got banged up. Sam didn't let go
until my Dad was down the street, and he got a
busted-up mouth and had to get stitches. This
incident traumatized me because there was a
lot of blood, and I realized my siblings did this
because they saw me do it all the time.

One time, I even thought about killing
myself. I can't remember what happened, but

I ran away from home, down the street to my friend's house, cried to his parents and told them it was not worth it and I was going to run out into the street and end it all. I don't remember how they talked me out of it, but they did.

My parents. Looking back, I realize my parents were not bad people. They did the best they could under the circumstances of being an immigrant family. My father was from North Vietnam and a relatively wealthy family. My mother, on the other hand, was from South Vietnam and a poor farming family, and because of this, my father's family did not approve of my mother, so there was tension all the time.

I cannot imagine the stress and fear my parents must have endured to abandon their home during a war with three small children, literally leave behind everything they owned except the clothes on their backs and move to a new country where they did not speak the language or know anyone. As time went on, my parents' marriage began to crumble. My father turned to alcohol, and my mother's bipolar disorder began to manifest itself.

Peter's childhood saddened me. While my family was not perfect, I never suffered or had to endure any of the things he had to. I often used Peter's childhood and the things he experienced during that time as an excuse for the things he did.

CHAPTER 5

Job Losses

Firing from a Computer Company

I REMEMBER THE THURSDAY MORNING Peter left to head to the corporate offices of the company he worked for because he was summoned there. We both knew he was going to be fired. His income and benefits were the only things we had as I was staying home with Brendan at the time. I hoped in my heart they would not let him go, but Peter had a history of making poor judgment calls, and he had been warned before by his employer.

I heard from him about two hours later, and sure enough, they had fired him. The story Peter told me about his being fired was that when he serviced one of the clients, they wanted some additional software for their computer system. Peter installed it and did not charge them for it. When he did the installation, something went wrong. Rather than tell his boss what he had done and get some help to correct the situation, Peter went back to the client's at one in the morning, talked his way through security, and tried to fix the mess he had made. The fix did not work, and when the office manager found out he had entered their office after hours without permission, she contacted Peter's boss. This resulted in Peter's being fired. I suspect this incident was really the straw that broke the camel's back as far as Peter's employment with this company as there were probably other things he did that contributed to his being let go such as his having porn on his company's laptop. My stomach was in knots, not knowing what we would do. We had no savings, nothing to fall back on. How would we survive? To my surprise, when he walked through the front door, he was not in the least upset and headed straight for the telephone. Peter had been telling me for a long time he could make more money if he was on his own, but I liked the safety of a steady job, steady paycheck, and benefits provided by the company.

By the end of the day, he had secured work as in independent contractor with one of the clients he serviced in the job he was just let go from and had also cut a deal with them to put us on their group health insurance. I have never seen anybody fired from their job and be as calm as he was, but his indifference allowed him to take immediate action rather than sit around being depressed. Over the next several days, he called most of the doctor offices he used to service and talked them into using him as an independent contractor to work on their computer systems. It did not take him long to build a lucrative business for himself. There were three computer engineers at his old job, but most of the clients who called in for service wanted Peter, not only because of his computer skills but, I think, more so because of his personality. Everybody likes him.

Our Franchise

The Pixar movie, *Cars*, was released in June 2006, and like all Disney aficionados, we saw it. During the movie, I was struck with the scenery of the West and had this epiphany we needed to take a trip out west. That did not happen until a year later. By then, Peter had been in his own computer business for several years, and the clients and business were drying up quickly. Neither he or I knew anything about running a small business, and because he had an instant client base when he was fired from his computer job which kept him busy for several years, we never did any marketing to obtain new clients for him.

By 2007, he had virtually no work, and no money coming in. We had enough unused Southwest Airline tickets to fly the three of us to Utah and good friends there who let us stay with them. Because of my epiphany, we decided to go for ten days. Our friends had a beautiful rancher in southern Utah, and the lower level was finished with three bedrooms, a full bath, formal dining room, living room, and eat-in kitchen. It was like having our own place. We rented a car and bought tickets to see several of the national parks—Zion, the Grand Canyon, and Bryce.

On our way back from Bryce, we stopped at a strip shopping center for lunch in a fast-food place. While eating, Brendan turned around and said, "Look, Mom, there's an embroidery store like the one back home." We had an embroidery store only ten minutes from our house in Maryland. It was a franchise. Years ago, while I was still working at the doctor's office, I had read a magazine article about a woman who had several embroidery machines in her home and made a good living doing embroidery while her kids were at school or sleeping. I was able to contact the woman, and she mentored me as I bought my own commercial embroidery machine and set up shop in our loft. This was another thing Peter supported me in, even though the machine cost as much as a car. Again, with no real knowledge of running a small business, I never made any money, only broke even. After two years, we sold the machine on eBay. I had loved running the machine, and Peter was artistic, so he helped in designing. Brendan even got into it, and we had made him all sorts of embroidered shirts. It broke my heart to get rid of the machine.

After finishing our lunch, we decided to go to the embroidery store and have vacation T-shirts made for us. As soon as we entered the store, I had this very strong "feeling" that I belonged there. We talked to the owner, who had not been open very long, and decided to investigate the franchise when we returned home.

Once back in Maryland, I contacted the franchise, and Peter and I met with one of their representatives. Everything and, I mean everything, fell into place, including the financing we needed to start the business. It was as if all of it was orchestrated by the universe.

After obtaining the financing needed (which included cashing out $110,00.00 in equity in our home and securing a line of credit for $60,000.00), attending two weeks of intense training at the corporate office in West Palm Beach Florida (Brendan's dad kept him for those two weeks), and corporate locating a storefront and setting up the store, we opened in January of 2008.

Our initial plan was for me to come in two days a week to pay bills and keep the books, and Peter would run the store. I was so grateful for this opportunity because it meant a new job for Peter with no background checks and no workplace rules for him to follow and then break and get fired—he was his own boss. With his artistic talents and his outgoing personality, I thought it a perfect set up. I even had dreams of building this business to the point we could sell it down the road, and it be our retirement.

Just as we opened with all our high hopes for this business, the economy started to take a dive and, eventually, crashed. I didn't know it at the time, but my father was dying, which meant trips to the ER, rehab facilities, finding him a nursing home, and cleaning out his apartment. He died the end of April that year. About a month after his passing, I realized Peter was not able to get out of the store and do any marketing. We had been trained it was critical to building up our business to go out every day from ten in the morning to noon and cold call businesses. I don't think Peter made it out of the store even a handful of times. I could not totally blame him. I saw running a storefront and two employees was overwhelming for him. Neither one of us had ever attempted anything like this before. It then became my full-time job to do all the outside sales and marketing and attend as many networking events each week as I could.

At first, I hated going out on the street every day cold calling. You had to be able to handle rejection and not take it personally. You had to be outgoing and able to talk to people and engage them in a conversation. You had to be able to be self-disciplined enough to follow up on all the businesses you visited and get appointments to go back and see whoever handled their apparel orders. I knew if I was going to be doing this the rest of my life, I needed an attitude adjustment. It was then that I started to read self-help, business, and personal development books and positive psychology books and have continued reading these types of books to this day. Through these books, I was able to change the way I looked at cold calling and networking and came to enjoy both. I met hundreds of people and was able to establish a large network. Some of these people became friends. I particularly enjoyed connecting people. No matter if you needed a plumber, handyman, lawyer, financial planner, a new job, etc., I knew someone who could help. I became very well-known in the hotel and hospitality industry in Baltimore City. We did business with major hotels and attractions in the city.

Peter and I loved our store, and he and I got along very well running it. Some couples find it difficult to work together, but we did not. Unfortunately, due to the economy, not getting out and cold calling until the business was into its fifth month, and the enormous cost of running the business, we were bleeding money in our first year and continued to do so. The rent alone was $4000.00 a month, and we went through all the $110,00.00 equity we had cashed out on our home in only twelve months. Looking back, we should have gotten out then, but we loved the business—it was our baby—and we thought, if we could hang in there, the economy would turn around, and we would be okay.

Next, we went through the $60,000.00 line of credit we had secured, both our pensions, and stock that had been set aside for my son's college tuition. We used credit cards, both business and personal, as well as credit extended to us by our vendors to keep going. One time, we were twenty-four hours away of being evicted by our store's landlord for back rent. Peter went to his parents several times for money, and they always gave us whatever we needed without expecting us to pay it back. I had enough gas and electric shut-off notices for the business and our house that I could have wallpapered a room in them. Several collection calls came in every day for bills we were behind on.

We were working six days a week, not taking any vacations, not maintaining the upkeep on our home, not buying anything extra, and never going to a movie or anything of that nature. We worked harder than either of us had ever worked and could not make any money.

There were other factors I believe which contributed to our failure.

Peter could not manage his time. He never had a plan for each day; he let the day run him. His famous line was that he had "fires to put out," so by the end of the day, the things he really needed to accomplish were left undone, and he would work late into the night, sometimes not coming home at all. I tried to help him with his lack of organization. I suggested he take one hour in the morning and close himself in the back office not to be disturbed by anyone; he would not even try it once. I suggested he pick two times during the day to check his email; he would not try that. Instead, he would get sucked in by his email and let more pressing things fall by the wayside.

Many times, he underquoted large jobs, and we would ultimately lose money on them.

He micromanaged our employees. He would even go so far as rearranging their workspaces to how he thought they should be set up after they had left for the day. When they returned the next day, they couldn't find their pens, pads of paper, notes they had made on orders, supplies to run the machines, etc. We had an amazing production manager who was with us from the day we opened until two months before we closed. He did not need Peter standing over him telling him how to do his job. He left us because of the financial instability of the store (he was not wrong) and because he could not deal with Peter any longer. I am surprised he stayed as long as he did.

The front counter position was like a revolving door. We had a few good people who knew their job and could work independently, but Peter would do the same thing to them, and they would leave. Sometimes, he made a few of them cry, and he would send them home for the rest of the day.

When Peter was stressed or under pressure, he was not fit to be around, and he would take his anger and frustration out on me in front of our staff. I was used to his outbursts, and while embarrassed that he did this in front of our employees, I let it roll off my back. I will never forget, after one of his outbursts, our production manager looked at me and said, "No man should ever talk to his wife the way he talks to you."

We had good times at the store. I grew to love going out and meeting new people. Peter was good with the customers who came into the store. Looking back, I think that was because he could schmooze them. Every Christmas Eve, we had a tradition of staying after the store closed, ordering pizza and wings, and making last minute gifts for our families. Brendan would stop by occasionally, and sometimes, he would help Peter after hours with an order because Brendan knew how to run the machines.

Over the five years we had the store, Peter and I tried to keep a positive attitude, but one day, in October of 2012 (right after our production manager quit), I knew I could not live like this any longer. I told Peter, and he agreed, so I called corporate and told them we could not go on and would have to close. They suggested selling the store and had someone who was interested in a franchise. I could not imagine who would buy an underperforming store, but this man and his wife did after they came by to look at the store.

We really did not "sell" our store. The new owner took over the store lease, the leases for the equipment, and the back royalties we owed. We stayed all night on December 31, 2012, to finish moving our personal things out. It was a bittersweet time; I had loved our store but was relieved to be rid of the stress and daily financial obligations we had not been able to meet for quite some time. I was embarrassed when, several months later, we had to file for personal bankruptcy. Until we opened the store, I had never in my life been late on a bill or flat out not paid a bill.

When we opened in 2008, there were approximately 400 embroidery stores worldwide. When we closed in December 2012, there were only about 200 stores left. Even those statistics did nothing to console me. I considered myself a failure, and I never really got over losing the store and filing for bankruptcy.

Firing from a Great Job

Peter had been working for the embroidery store near our house since we sold our store, but we knew that was a temporary thing until he found something else. It is hard to work in a place where you are not the boss after having your own business, especially when the business is the same as the one you used to own. After a few months at this store, it was obvious he was clashing with the owner more and more. I knew it was only a matter of time before she let him go.

Peter started working for a company downtown that promoted Baltimore city in May of 2013, handling their computer systems. This company is in a beautiful high-rise building in downtown Baltimore and is the marketing arm for Baltimore City, bringing conventions and events to the city. At the time, I was working in sales for one of the downtown hotels, and after Peter got this job, he and I became known as Mr. and Mrs. Baltimore because our jobs involved promoting the city. We had done several jobs for this company when we had our store, and I was well-known among the staff.

It was by chance Peter got the job. On the day we had to go to court for our bankruptcy hearing, we were early for the hearing, so we stopped by this company to kill some time. I jokingly asked the receptionist if they had any job openings, and she said they had one in their computer department. Peter filled out the application and was hired not long afterward. Of course, a background check was run, and Peter's criminal history was exposed, which included his armed robbery conviction when Peter was in his early twenties and the more recent theft from the hospital when we owned our store. I was embarrassed by this since I knew many of the people there and hoped those involved in the hiring process would keep this knowledge confidential. I have no idea how Peter explained his record. It is one thing to have done something when you were in your early twenties but another to have done something when you were in your forties, had a family, and owned a business. I felt he was hired because of my connections there, but of course, he said it was because of his schmoozing them in the interview.

While the pay was not high, the benefits were extraordinary. Health insurance and accrued time off, along with a pension, were some of the benefits that kept the company from having a high rate of turnover. The offices were beautiful, and there were many perks, such as a phenomenal Christmas party each year, free entry to many of the events that went on in the city, and the ongoing opportunity to meet new people and establish relationships. Peter seemed to be in his element.

Only a few months after he started working there, I was cleaning our house and saw some notebook papers on top of the cabinet we kept our DVDs in. I started reading them and saw they were notes Peter had made on many of the women he worked with—what they wore, how it turned him on, how he liked working underneath someone's desk while they were still sitting at their desk, etc. Most of these women were young, slim, and attractive. His notes hurt me deeply, not to mention the fact he didn't even take the time to hide them from me. When I confronted him, he said it was nothing, just something he did while sitting around one night. I was upset, but he gave me his usual statement when he pulls one of his stunts, "Why harp on something that happened yesterday. It's over, move on." I had to wonder how much time he spent lusting after the women he worked with every day. After some time, I let it go and chalked it up to his seemingly mental health issues that he was on medication for.

One evening in May of 2016, Peter told me he had to go back to the office to check on the computers after the burglar alarm had gone off. It was very late at night and seemed strange to me he would have to go as he was not responsible for security. The next day, I had a networking event to attend for my job, and Peter showed up at the event unexpectedly, telling me he took the day off so he could attend with me. At dinner that evening, he told me he had been fired the previous morning and didn't tell me right away because he did not want to ruin my day at the networking event. I was shocked! Peter's explanation was that some of the women at work did not feel comfortable around him, and he was let go because of that. There was another man at his office Peter had been exchanging inappropriate inter-office messages with about various women, and those messages were discovered. Peter was fired, but the other man was only suspended.

It did not make sense to me Peter was fired while the other man was only suspended. After some questioning, Peter admitted there was more, but he said he was not going to tell me what he did because he did not want me involved. He said if the company pressed charges, he would be going to prison—not jail but prison—for a very long time. He also told me since I was his wife, I was not allowed back in the building for any reason.

In addition to being worried about how we would pay our mortgage because Peter's entire months' pay went to cover our mortgage, I was incensed. I felt he had come into my circle of business acquaintances and friends and totally embarrassed me by his actions. This was another job loss that threatened our financial security. Not knowing what he had done deeply concerned me. I did not know if there was another arrest on the horizon, charges, more embarrassment, etc.

In the weeks that followed, he received several strange telephone calls and, at one point, told me he had to meet the security guard that worked at the building to pay him ten dollars to keep his mouth shut. Peter seemed truly nervous during this time, and I had never seen him like that. When the company cleaned out his office, he was so afraid he would be arrested if he went downtown to collect his personal belongings, he made me go and meet the HR person to pick them up. I told Peter that was ridiculous. If they were going to arrest him, they knew his address and would not have to wait for him to come back to the office. He was not "man" enough to get his things, so I had to drive downtown, meet the HR person (who I was friendly with), and get his personal belongings. I could barely look her in the face.

The day Peter got on the telephone with the unemployment office, he was told there would be no unemployment benefits for him because the company had fired him for sexual harassment, and there are no unemployment benefits for that. Peter admitted to the staffer at the unemployment office he had done the things the company put in the report. Apparently, whatever else he had done to result in his being let go, the company was keeping quiet about it.

CHAPTER 6

In Trouble with the Law

Banned from Our Local Movie Theater

IT WAS THE SUMMER OF 2003. We had just returned from a trip to California to visit my aunt and uncle. *Pirates of the Caribbean: The Curse of the Black Pearl* had been released, and we had seen it about four times. We even went so far as to decorate our family room in a pirate theme. Most of the rooms in our house had themes, and the family room was the last one to be done. Because we all love Disney so much, and the movie was amazing, we decided to go with that theme for our family room. Several items had been purchased in Disneyland to bring back for the family room, and it was shaping up nicely.

Peter and I went to see *The League of Extraordinary Gentlemen* at our neighborhood movie theater. Peter would go to the movies every day if he could. The movie theater was only five minutes from our house, so that was our go-to movie theater, and we went almost weekly. Peter left during the previews to use the restroom, but he was gone for what seemed like a very long time, so long that the movie had started. The next thing I knew, a security guard came down the aisle where I was sitting and asked if I would come with him. I said yes, and he took me to the manager's office on the second floor. Peter was sitting there with the manager.

The manager proceeded to tell me Peter took the *Pirates of the Caribbean* poster off the wall on the first floor and stole it! I was stunned. Peter admitted to taking the poster and putting it in our car. He said he thought the poster would look good in our family room. The manager was very nice. She said she sees us all the time at the movies and could not imagine why Peter had done such a thing. I couldn't either because, in addition to being illegal, the poster was way too big to fit on any of the walls in our family room, let alone get it out of the theater undetected. Fortunately, the manager said she would not press charges, but that we were not allowed in the theater ever again. I was wondering how I would explain to Brendan we could never go to the movies there since it was the closest theater to our home, and we went frequently.

On the way home, I asked Peter why he had done such a thing, and of course, he didn't know why. This stunt was beyond stupid, but at this point, I was getting used to him doing stupid things. I waited a week and went back to the theater alone to speak with the manager. I explained to her Peter was a refugee, had been abused as a child, and suffered from bipolar disorder which he was on medication for. I apologized again. To my surprise, she said after thirty days, we could return to the theater.

Copper Wiring

Brendan belonged to a very active Boy Scout troop, and every summer, the troop took a two-week camping trip. During those trips, I would fly to California to visit my aunt and uncle. I never felt relaxed leaving Peter to run the store and not have me around to try and keep him in line. The night I was to fly home, I had some time to kill in the airport, so I called Peter. He did not sound good and told me he had done something while I was gone. Since money was always an issue when we had the store, Peter had driven to the outskirts of Washington, DC, found a building that was under construction, went in, and took a bunch of copper wiring to sell. The building had security cameras, and Peter was caught. He had an appointment to go to the police station in a few days about the incident. Of course, when I returned, I went with him and tried to explain the usual—he had mental health issues, was on medication, etc. Thankfully, the police did not press charges, but we had to make restitution of over $1000.00.

The Hospital

On a beautiful spring day in 2010, I was leaving early in the morning to pick Brendan up from his father's, drop him at school, and head to our store. Peter was still getting ready to leave the house. I proceeded down our front steps to my car in the driveway. As I looked up, about eight men approached, and I could see several black cars parked in front of my house. The men identified themselves as Baltimore County Police detectives and asked me to go back inside the house. Once inside, they asked where Peter was and began searching the house. I waited in the dining room. The detectives would tell me nothing. Peter was brought downstairs in handcuffs. I looked at him and said, "What have you done?" He did not answer. The detectives took him. It is a miracle none of our neighbors saw him being taken away. I called Brendan and told him I was on my way. When I picked Brendan up, I had to tell him what had happened as he was sixteen at the time, and since I didn't know how long Peter would be in custody, I didn't think I could hide this from Brendan. I dropped Brendan at school and went to the store. I told our staff Peter was sick and would not be coming in. At the end of the day, I was notified by the police I could bail Peter out of jail. I did not have several hundred dollars lying around, so I had to humiliate myself and ask my ex-husband if he would loan me the money. Right away, he said that there was probably some sort of mix up, and Peter probably had not done anything. I told him that without knowing anything, I was sure Peter had done whatever he had been arrested for. Brendan and my ex-husband went with me to the county jail that evening to bail Peter out. As usual, Peter didn't seem very upset by any of this.

Several weeks prior, around 11:00 A.M., he had gone to a local hospital, parked his car in front of the hospital (his car had the name of our store and telephone number on it, and he had a jacket on with the name of our store on the back), walked into the women's wing, disconnected a computer from the wall, and left with it. That evening, he asked Brendan to bring the computer into our garage and set it on the workbench. We were always strapped for money, and Peter had intended to sell the computer. Unbelievably, after he stole it and brought it home, he forgot he had it and it just sat on the workbench. Peter always had spare computers and parts lying around the garage from when he had his computer business, so when I saw it, I thought he had moved it from another area in the garage. The computer was worth less than $1100.00. For Peter to help our financial situation, he would have had to rob a bank. I am glad he did not think about that, or else, he probably would have robbed a bank. This is a classic example of how Peter does not really think things through.

We had to hire a lawyer and go to court. Because the value of the computer was under $1100.00, his crime was considered a misdemeanor as opposed to a more serious felony, and he was sentenced to eight weekends in the county jail. Every Friday, I had to have him there by 5:00 P.M. and then pick him up Sunday evening at 8:00 P.M. For those two months, I lied to everyone at our church by telling them Peter's parents were going through some family issues, and he was spending those weekends visiting his family trying to help.

Our store had limited hours on Saturday, so customers could pick up their orders, and thankfully, our staff was not required to come in, so I didn't have to explain anything to them on Saturdays, but I had to go in on those Saturdays. I was not comfortable with our computer system because my role was outside sales, not front counter, but somehow, I managed.

By the time Peter went to court, was sentenced, and started serving his weekends, it was the holiday season. That year, Christmas Eve, Christmas Day, New Year's Eve, and New Year's Day fell on Saturday and Sunday, so he missed the holidays with us.

One of the Sunday nights, I picked Peter up from the county jail, he had a huge grin on his face when he got into the car and handed me $500.00 in cash. He was so proud of himself. He had smuggled some drugs into the jail for one of the other men who was also serving weekends. Peter said the man asked him to do it because Peter would not be suspected of anything like that since he had a family, lived in a nice neighborhood, and owned his own business. I could have killed him on the spot and could not believe he had done such a thing. Although, Brendan and I had a saying about Peter whenever he pulled one of his stunts: "Can you believe Peter did that? Yes!" "Can you believe Peter did that? No!" In other words, part of Peter's personality would never do such a thing, but the other part would. I took the cash and mailed it anonymously to a woman in my church who could really use it.

I later found out that video surveillance of him stealing the computer was shown to the employees in that building to see if anyone recognized him. One of the surgeons I used to work for had opened an office in that building with several of the women I had worked with. Someone in that office who knew us recognized Peter, and that was how he was caught. Talk about embarrassed! Even though I rarely had contact with any of these people, I was still seeing the doctor twice a year as a follow up to my breast cancer. After this, there was no going back to that office for me.

CHAPTER 7

Therapists, Psychiatrists, and Medication

IT BECAME OBVIOUS TO ME after only knowing Peter for a few months there was something not right with him. He lived in the moment, and I mean the moment—not years, months, weeks, or even days in the future. His world was what was right in front of his face at the time, and thinking about the consequences of his actions was not even on his radar. His driving was a prime example. I never knew anyone who drove with such recklessness as he did.

To say he was spontaneous would be a gross understatement. In the first couple of weeks he was my computer engineer when I worked at the doctor's office, I had a problem with one of our printers and had contacted him toward the end of the business day. At 11:00 P.M., he was on the telephone with me overnighting a brand-new printer without even looking at the one in my office that was not working. He later told me he got into big trouble with his boss for doing that. I think he wanted to impress me.

I convinced him to see a therapist with me. By now, we were a couple, and I felt if I was going to have a future with him, I had to find out why he did the things he did. We went to see the therapist I had used throughout my divorce. I had seen her for over two years, and she was excellent. After a few sessions with us, she felt Peter needed some sort of medication, and as she was not licensed to dispense medications, she referred us to a psychiatrist, and we began seeing her.

The sessions with the psychiatrist consisted of her asking Peter to talk about his childhood. I did not know many of the things he told us and was appalled by what he had been through and thought it was no wonder he had the issues he had and did the things that he did. She diagnosed him as having ADHD and put him on medication. Peter did not want to take any drugs, but he reluctantly agreed to.

This was all new to me. I did not know, with these types of drugs, it is usually by trial and error to find the right drug and then the right dosage. Peter is extremely sensitive to medication, and the medication that was supposed to take weeks to have an effect took only days. Some of the side effects were not pleasant. One drug he was placed on caused him to sweat profusely, which made him extremely irritable, and he had to be taken off that. After almost a year of seeing this psychiatrist, it seemed we were not making any progress; every session was the same. She would ask him to tell her a thought and then tell him to "go with that." She never really offered any answers or suggestions as to how to help him improve.

We then had Peter's medical doctor refer us to a different psychiatrist. After only a few sessions with him, he diagnosed Peter as having bipolar disorder and suggested we also see a therapist in his practice on a regular basis. He said Peter had been misdiagnosed by the first psychiatrist, and the drugs Peter had been prescribed by her were making his condition worse. Of course, we went through several more months of trial and error to get the right drug and the right dosage. In addition, he put Peter on a drug for depression. It also seemed Peter had a bit of seasonal depression disorder because almost every fall, when the days began to get shorter, I had to get his medications adjusted.

The poor man was like a walking pharmacy. I was concerned about all the medication Peter was taking and possible side effects that may not manifest themselves until months or even years later. While I was not elated to hear any of this, I felt relieved because now, I thought I knew why he did the things he did, and I hoped, with the regular therapy and medication, he would improve. Unfortunately, Peter would go off his medication from time to time, and I found this was typical for people with these issues. He would seem to stabilize, and once he felt better, he would stop taking his medications even though he knew he should remain on them. As time went by, I got better and better at recognizing when he went off his meds and could get him back on with less time of him being off them. Eventually, we were able to stop seeing the therapist and psychiatrist and have his medical doctor refill his prescriptions.

A friend of ours went out of town to learn to be an "energy healer." When she returned, she was looking for people to practice on. Because I never felt comfortable with Peter being on all this medication, I suggested to Peter he be a "guinea pig" for our friend and work with her for several sessions. I was hoping she could do something to get him off his medication and maybe even stop doing the things he did, but after several sessions with her, Peter became disinterested, and that was the end of that.

In the spring of 2016, we changed medical doctors because ours had retired. During Peter's check up with our new doctor, the doctor took Peter off Lamictal, which is the mood stabilizer Peter had been on for years to treat his bipolar disorder. I admitted to being a little bit nervous with Peter going off this medication but I also hoped he could stay off so he wouldn't be on so much medication. Two months later, I noticed no change in Peter being off the Lamictal. While I was relieved he was off it, I had to wonder if Peter had been misdiagnosed all these years and taking medication needlessly. This was a double-edged sword for me because I wondered if the suspicion way in the back of my mind, that Peter is a sociopath, was really the case, that there is no medication to help him, and that he doesn't want to be helped.

CHAPTER 8

Porn, Porn, and More Porn

PORNOGRAPHY WAS AN ISSUE EARLY on in our relationship even though we had a very active and, I thought, satisfying sexual relationship. My first recollection was the day one of the men he worked with at the computer company stopped by our house, and he and Peter openly discussed the fact their company had found pornographic images on Peter's company-issued laptop. I was appalled. After the man left, Peter explained to me that his laptop had become infected with a virus, and the virus caused the pornographic images to pop up on his laptop. I was not very tech savvy, and it was not until years later I realized it was the other way around—the virus would infect a computer because pornographic websites had been visited. I am sure the porn found on his company laptop contributed to his being fired from the computer company he worked for.

Another time, we had some friends over for an informal dinner at our house, and we were sitting around the kitchen table after eating. Our computer was in our kitchen, and suddenly, pornographic images popped up on the screen. Talk about being embarrassed, but Peter explained it away as our computer having a virus that he had not gotten around to taking care of.

I became suspicious and looked through our computer when he was not home. Even though I was not tech savvy, I found many pornographic pictures on our computer which I promptly deleted. When I confronted Peter, he said he didn't know why he did it, and he seemed truly remorseful, but it was as though he could not under-

stand the enormity of what he had done. He also could not understand why I was upset and hurt by this. It was a while before I could
continue having sexual relations with him. Again, his mantra was
that it happened yesterday, why harp on it; just move on.

Over time, I would get a feeling and start looking around
on our computer. Every time, I found pornographic pictures and,
sometimes, videos he had downloaded. I would say, over the years,
I deleted hundreds of these images. Sometimes, I would wake up in
the middle of the night and find him in the kitchen looking at porn
when he was supposed to be catching up on paperwork. Other times,
I would come into the kitchen in the morning and find the shades in
our bay window had been pulled down. I knew he pulled them down
because he had been viewing porn and did not want the neighbors to
see him, but he would forget to put the shades back up.

Another time I confronted him, he was adamant that Brendan
and his girlfriend must have been watching porn on our home computer. He was so convincing I asked Brendan, even though I knew in
my heart Brendan had not done it. Brendan was incensed Peter had
accused him, and I know this changed the way Brendan viewed and
felt about Peter.

One night, when I caught Peter looking at porn, he heard me
approaching and quickly cleared the computer screen, but I knew
what he had been doing. I still cannot believe he looked at me and
said this time he had been watching two guys "going at it," and did
I think he was gay? It was as if he had no clue to the magnitude of
the damage he was doing to our relationship. All he cared about
was if he was okay/normal. I didn't even give him a response to his
ludicrous question.

The worst incident with porn was on a Saturday during the time
we had our store. Saturdays, we had limited hours in the morning,
but Peter always managed to stay most of the day, and I would usually go in but stay only a couple of hours. On one particular Saturday,
I had attended an all-day family history workshop at our church and
told Peter I would come by the store after it was over at around 4:30
P.M. When I arrived, the front door to the store was unlocked. We
always locked the door after the store closed for the day. I found Peter

in the back at his desk watching porn and masturbating. On the floor was a small safe he kept locked under his desk. It was open, and I could see various sex toys inside. The door to the store had a buzzer on it, so every time someone came in, the buzzer would sound. He was so into what he was watching and doing, he had not even heard me enter. Seeing him like that sickened me to the point I thought I was going to literally vomit. I lost my temper, shouting at him and telling him we were through as husband and wife.

To my utter surprise, he broke down to the point it scared me. I thought he was going to hurt himself. Because of this, I calmed down and agreed to stay with him and try to work through his porn addiction, but this incident was what caused me to stop having sex with him. He was extremely apologetic, and I felt it was genuine, but I was done with any type of physical relationship with him. It was not meant to be a punishment, but after all the times I caught him watching porn and my spending hours deleting pictures and videos off our home computer, I just did not have it in me to be intimate with him. I still loved him and wanted to be his wife, but I was deeply hurt.

It took me a very long time to realize his porn addiction was not because of something I was lacking; it was because of something lacking in him. I realized this when I read an article about a famous movie actor who was in a relationship with a beautiful model and caught with a prostitute. I could not fathom how this man, who seemed to have everything—money, fame, and one of the most beautiful women in the world—could take up with a prostitute. That's when it hit me that it was not my fault Peter was into porn; it was a choice he made—something to do with him, not me.

CHAPTER 9

The Good in Him

The Little Girl in Sunday School

A LITTLE GIRL AND HER family moved to Baltimore in August of 2011. At the time, Peter and I were teaching primary and Sunday school for the six-year-olds. Primary is the time before Sunday school when all the children between the ages of four and twelve gather together to sing songs, give talks about the Gospel, learn Gospel principles, and make crafts.

I will never forget when this little girl was brought into the room. She was severely handicapped physically. She had been in a wheelchair since the day she was born and had difficulty talking because she has a trach tube in place. Everyone turned around to look at her as her parents wheeled her into the room. She looked so frail, her limbs so thin it seemed as if they would break at any moment from the slightest movement. Her skin was so pale as if she had not seen the sunlight in a very long time. Her head wobbled from side to side because she is unable to hold her head erect. Thick glasses rested on her nose.

There were two classes for the six-year-olds, and I remember wishing she would be placed in our class. The primary president looked at her, and before she could make a decision which class to put her in, I said we would take her in our class.

Immediately, Peter pulled a chair out of the middle of the row the children were to sit in and rolled her into that spot so she would have her classmates on either side of her rather than sitting on the end of the row. It made me think that she had probably spent her entire life sitting at the end of the row and never knowing what it is like to sit between others. Peter's action was instantaneous; he didn't even have to think about it. I would never have thought to do that. He wanted her to feel as though she belonged.

Because of her trach tube, one of her parents had to be with her at all times in case the alarm went off and an adjustment had to be made. After a couple of Sundays, Peter approached her parents, asking them to show him how to make any adjustments in her trach tube so that her parents could attend their classes.

Peter even made the effort to be able to understand her, and he always called on her in class. Most people who see her don't know how to respond or act around her. Peter treated her no differently from the other children in our class, and because of that, the children accepted her as one of their classmates. The love and compassion he showed to her seemed to come naturally to him, and because of that love and concern, we became very good friends with her and her family.

Peter always had a way with children of all ages but especially the ones that were "different." There was a boy in my Brendan's Scout troop who had been diagnosed with Asperger's syndrome. Once a month, the scouts would go on a weekend camping trip, and the dads were asked to help with the transportation to and from the camp site and to stay and camp with the scouts. None of the dads ever wanted this boy in their car because he talked incessantly and asked a lot of questions, but Peter always took him in his car. This boy's mother approached Peter and thanked him for taking an interest in her son, for making him feel wanted, and for helping to make his camping trips memorable and enjoyable.

Quitting My Job

It was August of 2011, and it was becoming more and more evident that my mother was not going to be able to continue watching Brendan. I really did not want to find someone to watch him or put him in day care before and after school while I was at work. Peter's solution was for me to quit my job. I had a very good-paying job with benefits, but I had always wanted to be able to stay home with Brendan. If I quit my job, our income would be cut in half, and I didn't know how we would survive, but Peter was insistent. He said it would all work out.

A couple of weeks later, we went to California for ten days to visit my aunt and uncle, and the day we returned, I handed in my resignation giving three weeks' notice. We never even sat down with a piece of paper to look at our finances, budget, etc. I simply wrote the resignation letter and handed it in.

The first week in October was the beginning of my being home for the next seven years. It wasn't until that first day home I realized Peter was now responsible for half of all of Brendan's expenses, including the tuition for the parochial school he was attending. I could not believe I had not thought about that, but Peter had always treated Brendan like Brendan was his own son.

We had to eliminate some things that were not essential, that is, cable TV, treatment for our lawn, shopping at nice stores, and a few other things. I had to make adjustments, but we did survive, and those seven years of being able to put Brendan on and off the bus, volunteer at his school, go on field trips, and being able to make my home and family my first priority were some of the best years of my life. I felt as though I was fulfilling a dream I had had for a very long time but never thought it would ever be realized. During that time, my mother became ill and eventually passed away, but I was able to be there for her because I was not working. I owe Peter a huge debt of gratitude for giving me those seven years with Brendan.

Home Depot and the Boogie

Brendan must have been around five or six years old. The three of us were in Home Depot one afternoon. I was looking at something and heard Brendan giggling behind my back. When I turned around, I was mortified! Peter had put Brendan on his back on top of a counter and was digging in Brendan's nose. I shouted at him, "What are you doing"? To which Peter replied that Brendan had a boogie in his nose, and he was getting it out. Yes, I was embarrassed. Peter should have asked me for a tissue and taken Brendan into the men's room to get it out. However, since I met Peter, he had always treated Brendan as if Brendan was his. One of the things that attracted me to Peter was the way he bonded with Brendan and treated him. Peter was constantly telling Brendan how much he loved him and kissed on him until he was almost twelve years old.

Flower Arranging

At one time, I had an interest in flower arranging and had taken a few courses at our local high school. Twice a year, we always attended a craft show, *Springtime in the Woods* and *Christmas in the Woods*. The show was held in an old Victorian house, and most of the items sold were handmade. I took some of my arrangements to the woman in charge, and she allowed me to sell them at the show. Because we had been attending the shows as a family for several years, she was familiar with us. As I was setting up my arrangements, she mentioned that we had attended quite often. I told her Brendan and Peter loved to shop. She made the remark, "Like father, like son." I asked her if she thought Peter was Brendan's father, and she replied she did. I asked her to look at them and see there was obviously no resemblance, and how could she even think they were father and son. Her remark was that because of the way she had seen Peter treating Brendan and interacting with Brendan, she thought, for sure, Brendan was Peter's biological son. I was amazed she would think that, and I felt grateful Peter was so loving with Brendan.

Taking the flower arranging courses and putting my designs on consignment at the craft show were just two of the things I wanted to do that Peter supported me in. No matter how much something cost or how much time was involved, I knew I never had to "ask permission" of Peter; it was okay with him. I always told everyone how Peter supported me in anything I wanted to do. Looking back, I came to realize he did not support me because of his love for me but because of his indifference toward me.

During the time Peter worked at the restaurant, there was another shift manager who lived forty-five minutes (by car) from the store. Currently, she had no car because it needed a new transmission, and she did not have the money for it. She walked, took the light rail and a bus to work which took her about two hours one way. One night, she got off at 10:30 p.m., and Peter offered to come back to work and drop her at the light rail station so she did not have to walk in the dark. We had taken her home, one night, last week. After talking about it, Peter said he was going to take her all the way to her house because he did not feel right dropping her at the light-rail station. About five minutes after he let her off at her apartment, she called him and asked if he could come back to her apartment because her gas and electric had been shut off (she was behind in the bill), and she wanted him to take her food and keep it in our fridge so it would not spoil.

Peter felt he could not leave her without electricity, in the dark, so he brought her (and her food) back to our house to stay in our guest room for the night. We took her to work the next morning for the 9:30 A.M. start of her shift. This is one of the things I love about Peter. He never looks down on other people because of their circumstances and is always willing to help. He really has a heart of gold.

In 1988, at the age of only thirty-one years old, I was diagnosed with breast cancer and had both breasts removed, with subsequent reconstruction. The plastic surgeon who placed the implants told me they would not last forever. Fortunately, I never had any problems with them until the summer of 2014 when, as I was brushing my teeth, I noticed the right side of my chest was considerably smaller than the left side.

It was discovered that implant had ruptured, and the other side contained a huge hematoma. Thankfully, one of the best surgeons skilled in the procedure I needed was only thirty minutes from my home. I needed extensive surgery which required three days in the hospital and the first twenty-four hours in ICU to monitor my progress. Even though, by now, Peter and I had been living as "roommates," he was beyond wonderful.

My surgery was on a Monday. Peter had recently missed two weeks from work for a shattered toe in a bicycle accident, so I did not want him taking the day off. I had Brendan drop me at the hospital in the morning, and Peter came by after work. Peter stayed with me the entire night, staying up to feed me ice chips all through the night, returning to work the following morning with virtually no sleep.

I came home from the hospital with four drains—two in each breast—and they had to be emptied daily. The drains had to stay dry the first few days. Again, Peter was wonderful to me. He emptied my drains, cleaned around the openings of the drains, and helped me bathe so as not to get the drains wet. He was patient, caring, and compassionate.

PART 2

A Fresh Start

CHAPTER 10

The Move to Florida

ABOUT A WEEK AFTER PETER was fired from his downtown job, Brendan called and said he had watched a program on TV about Walt Disney World, and he has decided to move to Florida to be near Disney because his best childhood memories are from our vacations to Disney. I was shocked but not surprised; Brendan was raised on Disney. I brought him home from the hospital dressed in a Mickey Mouse sweater along with a small plush Mickey that Brendan took with him everywhere until he was in middle school. Brendan still has his "Mickey" to this day.

In 1990, on my tenth wedding anniversary (before Brendan was born) Brendan's dad and I took a trip to Walt Disney World. From the moment I stepped onto Disney soil, I felt a connection, a sense of belonging, peace, and comfort that I could not explain. For me, Disney was more than a place to go on vacation and have a good time or relax. It was like a yearning for home, the reason animals migrate. Since that first trip, his father and I went back every year. Once Brendan was born, we would go in December for Brendan's birthday. I had begged Brendan's dad to move to Orlando, but he would have no part of it.

Before Peter and I married, I told Peter he had to promise to take me to Disney every year, which he did until we got the store and could no longer afford to go. Our last trip to Disney was in December 2008. On one of our vacations to Disney, we looked at houses, but because I had joint custody of Brendan with his father, moving out of state and taking Brendan with me was not an option.

My first thought after Brendan told me he was moving to Florida was how much I would miss him; he is my only child. I managed not to tell him that and, instead, told him if he was going to do such a thing, now was the time. Even though he had recently bought a cute little house and had been working at UPS for four years, he was not married and had no children. The next words out of his mouth were, "Why don't you and Peter come with me? It would be a fresh start for the two of you. Peter currently has no job, and the two of you can live with me until you get back on your feet." Peter was beside me listening in, and he agreed to move right on the spot.

Even though I had always dreamed of living near Disney and working there, Maryland had been my home my entire life, and I loved living there. We were close to Washington, DC, New York City, the ocean, the mountains, we had the change of seasons, we lived in a beautiful neighborhood with great neighbors, and I had many, many friends and acquaintances. On the other hand, I felt an urgency to get away and to make a fresh start somewhere else. Even though Baltimore is a major city, sometimes it is called Smaltimore because everybody knows everybody. I had no idea of the magnitude of whatever it was Peter had done to get himself fired from the company he worked for downtown and if it would ever become public knowledge. I also did not know who at that company knew what he had done and if the details of his firing would leak out to people we knew. I was ashamed and embarrassed to be his wife. I felt a resentment toward Peter because, by his actions, I felt he had taken away the network of people I had spent years building, some of whom had become friends.

About six weeks later, I lost my job because the man who owned the company could no longer afford to pay me. Since the position was an "outside service" position, there was no unemployment for me, and we were left with no income and no savings. Brendan had been driving for Lyft part time for a while, and he suggested Peter and I give it a try so we would at least have money for everything except our mortgage. Both of us applied, and within three days, I was driving for Lyft. Because of Peter's criminal record, he was turned down. Peter loves to drive, and this really got to him so much so that he told me point blank he resented the fact they hired me and not him. As I spent my days driving for Lyft, Peter was filling out applications for computer jobs in Florida with no results.

Through a friend of ours at church, Peter was able to get a job at Camden yards at the concession stands during the home baseball and football games. It did not pay much, and if the Orioles or Ravens were not in town, he did not work, but it was money coming in we did not have with him staying at home.

One night in August 2016, we went to a baseball game as spectators. Peter got a lot of free food from the stand where he worked, and he mentioned he gets free food while he is working, but it is not as much fun to eat while he works because the managers know they do it. He said it was more exciting before work sneaking food when the managers did not know. This statement gave me chills. Was he telling me doing the wrong thing excites him, and that's why he does these things?

Early in September, I woke up, and it was 1:00 a.m. Peter should have been home from his job at the concession stand at the ball game by now. I checked, and the game ended around 10:00 p.m. He stays one hour afterward to clean up. He took the car which meant it took about thirty minutes to get home. He should have been home no later than midnight. I texted him and got no reply. I called, and on the third call, he picked up. He told me he was on his way home and that one of the leads got fired, so he had to stay and count money and do inventory. There was something about his voice that told me he was lying. I was still awake when he got home. I questioned him, and he said what he told me was a lie, that he was sleepy when he got back to the car, so he set his phone alarm to wake him up at 11:30 p.m., but it never went off because he mistakenly had set it for 11:30 a.m. I asked why he lied, and he said the story about being a lead was a better thing to say. I wondered if there was something else that happened, and he was not being truthful. It deeply concerned me that he lies when it is not necessary, but he has always been that way.

A few days later, Peter left to visit his parents and two of his siblings for the weekend. It had not been a good week for us. He lost his job on May 12 and did not work at all until the middle of July when he picked up working at the concession stand at the games. The work was not steady; just when the Orioles or Ravens were in town. In the meantime, I had been driving six days a week for Lyft to try and keep us afloat. This week, there were no home games, which means Peter did not work all week. He had a list of things he wanted to get done for our upcoming move. He did none of them and basically wasted the entire week while I was out working. I felt myself becoming very resentful of him and his lack of contributions to our household.

Because we had one car, I was without a car the entire time he was gone, but I felt it important for him to visit his family. Once we moved to Florida, he would be too far away to drive to visit them and would have to fly to see them, which meant he would not be able to visit as often as he had been. Sunday night, I went to bed before he got home. I did not hear from him all weekend; he knew I was upset with him when he left on Friday.

Monday morning, when I got up, there was a note from Peter taped to the bathroom mirror, "I am sore, but wake me up at 6:00 or 6:30 a.m. to talk." I had no idea what that meant and was hoping he wanted to talk about his lack of help around the house and his inadequate attempts to find a steadier job until we moved. On the kitchen counter, I saw paperwork pertaining to a car accident and now realized he was in an accident over the weekend. As I headed outside for my morning walk, I told myself no matter how bad the damage was to my truck, I would not get upset. Imagine my surprise when I saw a car in our driveway I did not recognize! Now I knew the accident was bad. When I returned from my walk and woke Peter up, he told me he rammed into the back of another car on the highway less than a half hour after he left his parents' house to drive home Sunday afternoon. The car he hit was not badly damaged, but our truck could not be driven and was towed to the body shop where his sister worked. The car in our driveway was his mother's car, which he drove home. He did not know if our truck was totaled.

I contacted Lyft and found out I could only drive for them with a car that I owned or one of their rental cars, and right now, they had no rental cars available, which meant I could not work! Peter has managed to fix it so I couldn't work and bring any money in. Now we waited to find out if our truck was totaled. In the meantime, Peter had his mother's car to drive, and I had a rental car through our car insurance.

Even though we should not spend the money, we went to a fast food restaurant near our house for dinner that night. The shift manager happened to be a member of our church who we had not seen in quite some time. When she was active, we used to frequently give her a ride to church. I jokingly asked if they had any openings, and she said they needed shift managers and would give Peter's contact info to the area manager. She told Peter to go online and fill out an application. He did, and the next day, the area manager contacted Peter for an interview. Because Peter would be around money, his criminal record was an issue, but he met the area manager in person and was able to persuade the man to hire him full time. He would start at the restaurant in a couple of weeks. I was able to get a part-time job at a retail store near our house, so between the two of us, we made enough money to cover all our bills except the mortgage.

I was reading the book *Emotional Agility: Get Unstuck, Embrace Change, and Thrive in Work and Life* by Susan David, PhD. Page 37 talks about old, outgrown ideas and gives an example of a man who behaves as if he was still living his childhood traumas each day. I wonder if that was the case with Peter.

As I was reading about the difference between guilt and shame on page 72, I had an epiphany. The book states,

> Guilt is the feeling of burden and regret that comes from knowing you've failed or done wrong. It's no fun, but like all our emotions, it has purpose. In fact, society depends on guilty feelings to keep us from repeating our errors and misdeeds. A lack of guilt is actually one of the defining features of a sociopath.

I had often wondered over the years if Peter is a sociopath. The book goes on to say,

> While guilt is focused on the specific misdeed, shame is a very different animal. Linked to the feeling of disgust, shame focuses on a person's character. Shame casts one not as a human being who did a bad thing, but as a human being who is bad. This is why people who are shameful often feel diminished and worthless. It's also why shame rarely leads us to take action to make amends. In fact, studies show that people who feel shame are more likely to respond defensively, perhaps trying to escape blame, deny responsibility, or even pin it on others. In studies, prison inmates who exhibited shame at the time of the incarceration ended up reoffending more often that those who exhibited guilt.
>
> The key difference between the two emotions? Self-compassion. Yes, you did something wrong. Yes, you feel bad about it, because, hey, you should. Maybe you even did something really wrong. Even so, this transgression does not make you an irredeemably awful human being. You can make amends, apologize and get to work paying your debt to society, whether that means sending flowers or serving time. You can strive to learn from your mistakes and do better in the future. Self-compassion is the antidote to shame.

This tells me what I had been wondering all along. Why does Peter do bad things and not learn from them? Why does he make the same mistakes over and over? I know he is not stupid. These few paragraphs have been huge for me as far as trying to understand my husband and why he acts the way he does.

More from the book on page 171:

Coherence—like familiarity and accessibility—is a crude proxy in our brain for "safe," even when the desire for coherence leads us to go against our own best interests. For example, numerous studies have shown that people who think poorly of themselves prefer interacting with individuals who also view them negatively. And it may astonish you to hear that people with low self-esteem tend to quit their jobs more often when their earnings increase over time. In their minds, it just doesn't seem coherent to be appreciated and rewarded. More logically, workers with healthier self-esteem tend to leave their jobs sooner when they don't get appropriate raises. For these people, it doesn't make sense not to get the reinforcement they feel they deserve.

It's the comfort we take in the familiar and the coherent that leads us to continue seeing ourselves based on how we saw ourselves as children. How we were treated as children is then used by us as adults to predict how we'll be seen and received today, as well as how we deserve to be treated, even when it's derogatory and self-limiting. By the same token, information that challenges these familiar and therefore "coherent" views can feel dangerous and disorienting, even when the disconfirmation shines a new, positive light.

Fear of success, or fear of even being "okay," can lead to self-sabotage, including underperformance in school, being a slacker, or ruining an otherwise healthy relationship because you haven't "earned" it.

Many years ago, when the two of us were in therapy, our therapist mentioned that Peter sabotages himself and his world because he doesn't think he deserves a "good life." I can certainly see this. Although he loves to work, he has gotten fired from every job he has had since I have known him and for deliberate actions on his part that he knew were not right.

Toward the end of September, I woke up at 1:30 a.m., and Peter was not home from working at the stadium. I checked the Internet and saw the game had ended at 9:30 p.m. I called him twice, and he did not pick up. Finally, he called me back and said he was on his way home. He told me the people he worked with had given him a going-away party since it was his last night working there, and they had pizza and sat around and talked. I had a very hard time believing he had formed enough of a relationship with these people (he worked with different ones on different nights depending on which stand he was assigned to) to warrant a party and it taking two hours to eat pizza and talk, not to mention the fact we had to get up for church the next morning, and now it was very late. Trusting Peter had always been an issue. I didn't know if he was doing something else or had just exercised poor judgment and lost track of the time, which he did frequently. I will never know. I suspected, in this case, he was not telling me the truth-again.

The end of the following month Peter had left for his 9:00 a.m. shift at the restaurant, and I was ready to leave for my afternoon shift. I had closed all the tabs on the computer. When I came into the kitchen to get my keys, I noticed that Peter's Outlook was open, and I had no idea how that happened. When I approached the computer to close it out, I saw extremely pornographic videos that had been emailed to Peter by some porn site. He had placed them in various folders and even red flagged some of them. They went back to the beginning of the year and were as recent as October 3.

This was not the first time we had issues over his porn addiction. When I got home from my shift, I confronted him, and of course, he tried to lie his way out of it saying they were spam and sent to him, but the fact that the bottom of them had an unsubscribe option, and he was still subscribing, showed he was lying. It was so hard for me to believe he was still doing this. Of course, he looked and seemed remorseful and said he was sorry, but this had been an issue between us since the day I met him.

I was always trying to understand him and was now reading *The Psychopath Whisperer: The Science of Those Without Conscience* by Kent A. Kiehl. While Peter seems to have some of these tendencies, I refuse to believe he is a psychopath. I wonder why he continues to have poor judgment and not learn from his mistakes. We must go to court the day after tomorrow for the accident he had last month in Virginia in which he totaled our car. The lawyer who would be accompanying him to court suggested Peter take a safe-driving class to show the judge he is trying to do better. I can't tell you how many of these classes he had taken in the past. The course is online, takes eight hours to complete, and has to be done twenty-four hours prior to your court appearance so they can get the certificate in time for you to take it to court. When would Peter begin the course? He would start Monday night around 8:00 p.m., which meant he had to stay up all night to get through the course and take the exam. Peter's reading comprehension has never been good, and he is a slow reader. He has known for over two weeks he needed to do this, so he waited until the last minute to get it done.

In the meantime, the insurance company determined our car was totaled. It is by the grace of God our car was valued at a few hundred dollars more than what we still owed it on. I scrambled to find us another car.

Peter and I had to travel to Virginia for court for his car accident. Because he had to take his mother's car back to his parents' house, I had to follow him in our car and bring him back. Since he had a clean driving record and took the driver education class, everything was dropped, and there were no points on his license and no fine. Another miracle as far as I am concerned.

Once home, Peter and I watched a TED talk given by Tali Sharot on "optimism bias." I had never heard the term before, but the definition is: optimism bias (also known as unrealistic or comparative optimism) is a cognitive bias that causes a person to believe that they are less at risk of experiencing a negative event compared to others. This was another epiphany for me in trying to understand Peter. This explains why he thinks he will never get another speeding ticket or have another car accident or why he always underestimates the amount of time it takes to go someplace or get something done.

Brendan applied for and was granted a transfer to Lakeland, Florida, for his job at UPS. The area he was looking to buy a house in was halfway between Lakeland and Walt Disney World. His targeted move date was the beginning of September, but it took much longer to sell his house than expected. We did not actually move until the beginning of December. Brendan and I had flown to Florida for a day in October to look at houses. Fortunately, he had an excellent realtor who showed us fourteen houses, one of which Brendan bought. Peter and I were beyond blessed because both the store I was currently working at and the restaurant where Peter now worked agreed to transfer us to stores very close to where we would be living in a small town called Eagle Lake. Neither one of us envisioned working these jobs forever, but this afforded us some sort of income once we arrived in Florida.

The actual move was much harder than anticipated. I had been begging Peter for months to go through his things and weed out what he was not taking with us. Peter has always been sort of a hoarder. He had computer parts and devices in our garage that were going on fifteen years old and beyond obsolete. He had several boxes from his downtown office with mugs, pens, lanyards, etc. that he never even looked at once I picked his personal things up after he had been fired.

Peter picked up the moving truck on a Thursday. It was the biggest one we could get without needing a special driver's license. The plan was to load it Thursday and leave some time on Friday. Brendan left Friday afternoon since he had to be at work in Florida on Monday morning. Even with help from our friends, we did not finish loading the truck until late Saturday night. I had to give away some furniture and other things I wanted to take because there was just no room. The truck was packed and probably over the weight limit. My Ford Escape was packed as was Brendan's Mustang which we were towing behind the moving truck.

Peter and I rolled out of Maryland at 5:00 a.m., Sunday morning, and did not arrive at Brendan's house in Florida until 5:00 a.m., Monday morning. We had to go below the speed limits because the truck was so full. We only stopped twice, each time for a thirty-minute nap. I consider it a miracle we arrived and in one piece. Fortunately, people from our new congregation showed up in the afternoon and worked into the evening to unload the truck. Brendan's house had a large storage shed in the backyard, and if not for that, I don't know where we would have put half our boxes.

Since I was working part time, I was able to spend most of my time organizing and unpacking the things we needed. Most of our things would stay in boxes until we found our own place. I was pushing Peter to find a computer job that paid more than what he was making at the restaurant, but he seemed satisfied to stay at the restaurant. Peter was never one to look to the future; he only saw what was immediate and right in front of his face. I landed an interview for a call center that was full time, had benefits, and paid more than my current job. Even though the pay was less than what Peter was making at the restaurant, he felt this was a better opportunity, so he also applied but was turned down due to his criminal record. Again, he resented the fact I got the job, and he did not.

My training was six weeks, and into the first week, I saw this was not a place I wanted to be for various reasons. Right before the training ended, I interviewed and was hired as an admin at a real estate office. The money was the same, but it was much closer to home. I had bought a car when I got the job at the call center because there was no way I could work there full time and drive thirty minutes to and from work and share a car with Peter. The miracle was that when I went in to buy a car, I had mediocre credit, no money to put down, and was, technically, between jobs. I had left the retail store and was starting my job at the call center the next day, but I was able to get the loan and purchase a brand-new car.

Once again, the job at the real estate office was not a good fit for me, and the owner fired me just six weeks after I started. It was a relief to be let go, and for some reason, I had a feeling of peace and knew I would not be unemployed very long. It was not my nature to job hop, and I longed for job stability. When talking with Brendan, he suggested I apply to Disney. Even though I had always dreamed of working at Disney, I knew I would probably have to work nights, weekends, and holidays. My biggest fear was not being able to attend church on Sundays. I decided to see what played out and went online and applied for a part-time job opening in food services.

Within days, I had an interview and was beyond excited. I expressed my concern about working Sundays during the interview and was informed at that time part-time cast members pick the three days they want to work. I gave my availability as Tuesdays, Wednesdays, and Thursdays. At this point, the interviewer told me she realized I have no experience in food services. My heart sank, thinking I would not be hired. Next, she told me she saw by my resume I have retail experience and asked if I would be interested in working on Pandora in the gift shop. Pandora was the new land opening in Disney's Animal Kingdom in less than two months. Of course, I would be interested! I left the interview in a daze. I think I even floated out to my car. In exactly one month after being fired from the real estate office, I was sitting in Traditions, the one-day class every cast member attends as their orientation to working for Disney.

The next few weeks of training were a whirlwind. Pandora opened the end of May 2017 and was and still is a huge success. I could not believe I was offered a role there and became a part of Disney history. We had such an amazing opening team, and I grew to love the people I worked with. Everyone looked out for and helped one another as this was a new experience for each of us. I opened my availability to include Monday through Friday, so I had the weekends off and could attend church. I worked nights until 2:00 a.m. but loved it.

Peter and Brendan saw how much I enjoyed working for Disney. Peter decided he wanted to be a bus driver for Disney and applied. After five years of working for UPS, Brendan had become disillusioned with them, and he applied for a bus driver position as well. Brendan was hired and began his training in June. Peter went through a lot of back and forth with Disney over most of the summer about his criminal record and, ultimately, was denied employment. My being hired by Disney and then Brendan being hired for the position

Peter wanted did not sit well with Peter. He could not be happy for either one of us as he had his heart set on working for Disney. I don't think Peter realized that being turned down for jobs was because of poor choices he had made that landed him in trouble with the law. Brendan and I had never been in trouble with the law or had criminal records, and that was why we were hired, and Peter was not.

Once Brendan got into buses, he wanted me to transfer to buses, but I did not want to be full time for fear of not being able to attend church, and I did not want the responsibility of driving the guests.

However, I had this very strong feeling that I needed to go full time not only for more money but for the benefits. At the time, all my benefits were with Peter's job at the restaurant. I tried to ignore this feeling, but it was very strong, so at the end of August, I applied for a transfer to buses full time.

Around this time, I found out my house in Maryland would go to foreclosure. I felt it was my fault. I should have called the mortgage company the minute we decided to move to Florida and told them we were moving and try to work something out with them. Because of my fear it would sell before we were ready to move and leave us with no place to live, I never contacted the bank about our circumstances until we knew exactly when we were moving. By then, it was mid-November. I engaged an excellent realtor to sell the house, but he was not able to sell it. Losing this house was another major event in my life I would never get over. I had bought the house after I left Brendan's father and before Peter and I were married, so the house and the mortgage were in my name. The foreclosure went on my credit report, resulting in my not being able to get a mortgage for three years after the house was auctioned off by the bank. The auction did not take place until about a year later, in September 2017.

A few days later, while trying to log into my work schedule, two pornographic sites popped up in the history. I confronted Peter about this in the afternoon, and he told me he sometimes watched movies on this computer and the sites popped up, and he clicked on them by accident. I would not believe that story if I told it myself! I asked him how many times porn had been an issue in our relationship, and he admitted it's been an issue many, many, many times. I told him he was not only endangering our marriage, but if Brendan found out, he may want Peter out of his house. This was not the same as having our own home like we did in Maryland. I left it at that.

Around 2:00 a.m., I got up to use the bathroom. The light in the computer room was on. I opened the door and caught Peter watching a pornographic video! I could not believe it! We had a very serious conversation about this earlier, and he was at it again. I was going to have to do some real hard thinking about staying married to him because it was obvious he was not going to give this up.

The next morning, I found a note from Peter when I got up for work saying to wake him up before I left as he wanted to talk to me. I did, and he mumbled something about not telling Brendan and that we should discuss his porn problem with our bishop. I told him we have discussed this with every bishop we have ever had, and I was not going to waste this bishop's time or mine discussing it.

Mid-October, I went to casting for my department of transportation paperwork. I entered and saw Peter there filling out his paperwork. When I met the woman who was going over the paperwork with me, it was obvious Peter had talked to her and told her we were married and that Brendan is a bus driver. I was embarrassed and ashamed again to be his wife because this woman obviously now knew about Peter's criminal record.

While driving to work, I realized I did not want to be married to a man who repeatedly lies, gets into trouble with the law, cannot hold a job, and views pornography. Any one of those things is reason enough, in my opinion, to dissolve a marriage. There is a pattern to how Peter lives his life. After years of doctor visits, reading books and articles, I finally realized it is not my job to figure out why he does the things he does. Peter obviously does not want to change, or he would have by now. You cannot want something more for someone than they want it for themselves. I didn't know how this was going to play out, but I did know I did not want to spend the rest of my life with this man. I had spent most of the time we've been married feeling more like Peter's mother than his wife, always cleaning up behind him when he gets into trouble, or apologizing when he says something he should not say or gets himself into a situation. I was always wondering when the next incident would be—whether it was only saying something inappropriate or embarrassing, doing something illegal, or losing his job. It did not cross my mind that if Peter and I divorced, I would have no hope of moving out of Brendan's house. I had no savings and would be without Peter's salary. Why it had taken me twenty years to realize I do not want to be his wife, I do not know. Perhaps there were things I needed to learn along the way.

A few days later, I told Peter I wanted a divorce—that last weekend was the last straw. He looked at me with innocence and asked me what happened last weekend! I reminded him about the porn and that I told him when we moved here, if he pulled one more stunt, we were through. I even gave him a second chance last weekend when I saw the porn sites on the internet history, but several hours later, I caught him viewing porn again. He could not explain how he could do that. He did say because we had no sex life, he watched porn rather than having an affair; it's to save me from that! I reminded him he was viewing porn when we had a very active sex life. He then said he has a sex problem—he can never get enough. There are programs in our church that are free to help with that, but he said nothing. It was obvious he did not have any desire to change his ways. He told me he has other issues—referring to his getting into trouble with the law.

I suggested we dissolve the marriage—he doesn't even have to tell his family. Peter has always been about appearances. I told him I think I was nothing more than a trophy wife to him. He said nothing. I told him he could continue to live here are long as Brendan was okay with it. It was not my intention to hurt him or make things difficult for him. I wanted a life with him but do not want to feel the effects of his poor choices any longer. I do not want to be tied to him temporally or spiritually. It was obvious he would rather take the easier road and give in to his issues and addictions rather than get some help and try to work through his issues. I hold no bad feelings and feel very sorry for him. He said he would no longer attend church once we divorce. I could not tell if he was serious or trying to be funny. I found out later his downloading pornographic websites blew out Brendan's router and modem to the tune of $600.00 to replace them.

Peter had a day off and spent the entire day digging boxes of my good dishes and crystal out of the shed. We had a very pleasant evening unboxing, washing dishes, and putting the dishes and crystal in the china cabinet. We also put out some Halloween decorations inside the house. He even helped with the laundry, and we had time to watch a movie before going to bed. During the evening, he asked if I was really going to file for divorce. I told him after some brief research on the internet, it is quite easy to file in Florida and doesn't take that long for the divorce to become final. He looked as though he was sad, but when I asked if it was still okay with him for us to divorce, he said, "Whatever."

Since we moved to Florida, I had not found anyone to cut my hair the way I liked. Peter had been pestering me literally for years to let him cut my hair even though I had someone in Maryland I had gone to for over twenty years and was more than happy with. I had finally relented and allowed Peter to cut my hair. Despite the fact he had no experience cutting hair, he did an excellent job. While Peter was cutting my hair one afternoon, I jokingly asked him what I owed him for the haircut. He told me a night out. Like an idiot, I thought he meant a night out with me, but when I asked him, he said he wanted a night out with his friends. Later in the evening, when I thought we were going to watch a movie at home, he said he wanted to go night fishing with a high school kid he worked with. Peter had told me in the past this kid's father did not let him out at night, but now he can go night fishing?? I told Peter I didn't particularly believe him and asked him not to go. He said he had not done anything fun all day and wanted to go. He was supposed to work today but was given the day off because they were slow. I made it clear I would be very upset if he went, but he told me he would not stay out late, and off he went. He did not get home until 1:15 a.m., so I was not sure what he considers late.

Not long afterward, I tried to have a serious talk with Peter about our relationship. He told me he did not want to be married anymore, and when I asked him if he still loved me, he said he didn't. I asked why he did not want to be married, and at first, he said he doesn't know. When I pressed him, he said it's like the movie *The*

Sixth Sense in that he was not ready to tell me yet. I asked if there was someone else, and he said no. We printed the divorce papers off the internet and filled them out for a "simplified dissolution of marriage." We had yet to tell Brendan we were divorcing.

The three of us spent time cleaning out a closet several days later, and while I did not plan to say anything, I told Brendan we were divorcing. At first, he thought I was joking, but we let him know this was no joke. I felt I owed Brendan some sort of explanation as to why we were divorcing, so I told him about the porn. Brendan asked Peter how he could help him; that is, put parental controls on the computer. Brendan suggested Peter go for some sort of counseling. My heart ached for Brendan because, even though Brendan was an adult at this point, Peter had been very much a part of Brendan's life since he was four years old, and I knew our divorce would hurt Brendan. After much discussion about the issues in our marriage, Peter admitted he is "done." Brendan thought because Peter had not gotten the job at Disney, Peter was depressed and willing to give up on everything, including being in our family. The three of us decided to put the whole divorce issue on the back burner until after the holidays. That would give me time to get through my training to be a bus driver and Peter to find out if Disney would hire him as a bus driver.

Peter and I watched a Christmas movie together one evening. At 7:30 p.m., I told him I must go to sleep to get up early for training. He announced he was going out but didn't know where. When I pressed him, he said he was going to work to hang out. He hated his job and continually griped about the people he worked with, so why would he do that? When I left for work at 4:15 a.m., he was still not home, and I had not heard from him.

I got home from work, and Peter acted like nothing had happened. He mentioned Brendan looked upset when he went to work, so I told him Brendan was upset because Peter did not come home last night. Peter said he went to work, and a couple came in and invited him to their house for a party in Lakeland. He went and lost track of the time and did not want to drive home late. I found that hard to believe, and the worst part is that he didn't think he did anything wrong by staying out all night and not letting me know he was okay.

CHAPTER 11

Sociopath?

HOW IS IT POSSIBLE TO live with someone, love someone, and be with them most every day for years and not know if the things they do are because they have mental health issues that they cannot control, or if they are inherently a bad person? This is the question I had been searching for an answer to ever since I met Peter so many years ago. How can someone be so warm and loving and then turn around and lie, steal, and seem not to care about who they hurt or the feelings of those affected by their actions? There seemed to be no remorse or guilt in Peter.

After so many doctors, medications, and second chances, I am convinced Peter is a sociopath. There is no other explanation. His apologies were less and less sincere each time he pulled one of his stunts. Toward the end of our marriage, he didn't even bother to apologize for the things he did. I don't recall him ever telling me he would not repeat the things he did.

We are taught in church that "All are born with the Light of Christ, a guiding influence which permits each person to recognize right from wrong. What we do with that light and how we respond to those promptings to live righteously is part of the test of mortality." How could this man sit in church week after week, month after month, and year after year and not change his ways? How could this man be so active in his church, that is, volunteering his time at the church in various church positions, helping people move in and out of our area, doing service for anyone who was in need, and not want to stop doing the things he was doing? I thought if he went to church long enough, he would change his ways, but that did not happen. Peter told me whatever it was he did at his downtown job that was illegal and got him fired had been going on for months. That means, while he was a counselor in the bishopric in our church, he was carrying out illegal activities.

Peter did all the right things for all the wrong reasons. It is not my place to judge Peter, but I find it hard to believe he cannot help the things he does, and that he does not know right from wrong. I could not live like that any longer. I didn't deserve to live like that.

For a very long time, I thought if only I were more patient with him, if only I had done more to help with his mental health issues, I could have helped him. It took me years to realize he didn't want to change his destructive tendencies. What if he had? Then things would have turned out very differently for us. I never expected him to swoop in and make my life perfect. I never expected to be wealthy, live in a mansion, have fancy cars, travel the world. All I wanted was a normal life, to have the basics—a home and a family. I know life comes with challenges, but the ones Peter caused should have never happened.

CHAPTER 12

Brendan and Peter

As told to me by Brendan:

PETER CAME INTO MY LIFE when I was four years old and my first memories of him were going to his apartment and seeing all the candy canes he had hanging from the chandelier in his dining room. My mom and I would go to his place and swim with him in the pool at his apartment complex. He had not yet met my dad, and I was not sure how my dad would react once he knew about Peter. I told my mom it would probably be like the water in the pool. When you first get in, the water feels cold, but after a few minutes, you get used to it, and the water feels good. I thought Peter meeting my dad would probably not go well initially, but gradually, after my dad got to know Peter, he might like him, like adjusting to the water temperature in a pool.

I didn't mind having a stepdad because, in my early years, Peter seemed to be a good one. He was fun to be around, and he was always interested in me and what I was doing. He supported me by coming to my school events and participating in my Boy Scout troop. As I got older, all my friends liked him too. Most of the time, Peter acted like a kid, and that's why we had so much fun together.

The best times were the annual vacations we took to Walt Disney World as a family. From the time I was five years old until I was about fifteen years old, we went every year, and those trips were the memories I cherish most of my childhood. We had to stop going because once my mom and Peter had the embroidery store, they were no longer able to afford vacations.

Around age fifteen was when I started having suspicions and feelings that Peter was not the person I thought he was. Those suspicions and feelings became reality when I caught him several times viewing pornography, either in our home or at the embroidery store he and my mom owned. One of the times I caught him at the embroidery store, he tried to blame it on the production manager, but I knew better. Not long afterward, he stole a computer from a hospital, and that solidified in my mind he was not the person I thought he was. I knew then something was very wrong with him. Being very active in church did not stop Peter from swearing like a sailor whenever my mom was not around. Swearing the way he did, stealing, and viewing pornography did not go hand in hand with regular church attendance in my eyes.

I spent a lot of time at the embroidery shop, and while it may have seemed I was just a kid hanging out, I saw what went on. Peter treated the employees terribly, and I blame Peter for the failure of that business. There were times he would send someone home because he had made them cry.

I did learn from Peter to try and help others whenever I could because I saw Peter always helping people. He went out of his way to assist people at church, our neighbors, and our friends, but I later realized he did it for the wrong reasons. His motives were purely to receive praise and recognition. After growing up with Peter as my stepdad, it is my opinion Peter is nothing more than a con man. Because of knowing him, I am more cautious and vigilant of who I allow into my life and people in general.

CHAPTER 13

Norm

ABOUT THREE WEEKS AFTER APPLYING for the transfer to buses, I stopped by costuming on the way to my shift at Pandora. I stopped there almost every day on my way to work to use the restroom; my mom always said I have a bladder the size of a pea. This day, there was a bus driver sitting on the bench outside of the building. I knew he was a bus driver by the costume he was wearing. At this point, I was starting to wonder if I was ever going to be called about the bus driver role. I knew they desperately needed drivers, but it had been three weeks since I applied, and I had this sense of urgency to get the role. I explained my situation to him, and he told me not to panic. He assured me I would hear from them. Typically, I do not remember names unless I make a real effort to do so, but for some reason, I had a feeling I should remember his. His name was Norm, like the Norm on *Cheers,* and that was how I would remember his name.

A few days later, I stopped by again to use the restroom, and Norm was sitting on the same bench with another bus driver. I found out they were trainers, and they were waiting for people who were testing that day. Both Norm and the other trainer had been Brendan's trainers, and they remembered him. Again, I was reassured I would receive a telephone call about my transfer to buses.

Not one week later, I decided to take my break at Pride Rock (I never went there) and get a sub. I sat down at the table, looked up, and Norm was eating his lunch. I told him I still had not heard anything. I know I looked and sounded desperate, and he must have thought I was some sort of nutcase, but he assured me in his calm way I would hear something.

It was now almost the end of September. A few days later, I did receive a telephone call, and things were set into motion for my transfer which included a physical. I had already taken several written tests at our local motor vehicle office and had my CDL learner's permit. I passed the physical not long afterward, and on November 6, I started my six weeks training. Peter was to the point of being told no by Disney; they would not hire him, so he was not happy for me. It did not help that Brendan had been in buses since June. The six weeks of training consisted of learning to pre-trip the bus, skills, driving, and learning property. Some of the hours were days, and some were nights. Norm was a day trainer, and I would see him at the beginning of the day when I trained days, during our lunch hour, and at the end of the day. I had several trainers but never had him.

Less than two weeks into my training, I cut a right-hand turn too quickly, ran over the curb, the bus rocked, hit a stop sign which took some of the trim off the sign and left a faint red mark on the side of the bus. There was no disciplinary action since the damage was minor, and I was still in training. Of course, I felt terrible and was very embarrassed and wondered if I should be in buses at all. At the end of the day, as I was getting into my car, I looked up, and Norm had pulled his truck in front of my car. He came over to my window and asked if I was okay. He reassured me things like this happen, and it in no way means I should not be in buses. I could not believe he took the time to stay after and wait for me to see if I was okay.

I had mentioned meeting Norm to Brendan, and he remarked what an excellent trainer he is and how much he enjoyed having him for a trainer. He said Norm was divorced and just coming out of a bad relationship. I immediately felt bad for Norm. In the small amount of time I had known him and the few short interactions I had with him, I felt he was a kind, gentle man.

A day or two later, Norm and I happened to sit next to one another on the lunch bus. I mentioned Brendan had told me he was exiting a bad relationship, and that perhaps I could help him find someone if he could tell me his idea of the perfect woman. He looked at me very seriously and said I was his idea of the perfect woman. I laughed at him and said he didn't even know me, and I was boring; that is, I don't smoke, drink, swear, watch R-rated movies, or sleep with someone unless I am married to them. I then asked Norm what he was doing for Thanksgiving. Norm said he had no place to go. It was always our family tradition to invite people who have no place else to go for the holidays over to our house for dinner, so I invited him to our house. He declined as he did not want to leave his brother alone. I told him his brother was welcome too. Norm had to work on Thanksgiving, and we were eating at noon but said he and his brother could come after he got off work.

A few weeks before Thanksgiving, I attended a Sunday school class, and the topic was marriage. I had told myself numerous times over the years that if my marriage to Peter did not work out, I was finished with marriage, relationships, and men—done! Something happened during that class; another epiphany if you will. I had this strong feeling I must be open to another relationship. I told Brendan about this feeling and his immediate response was I should consider Norm. I told him I see Norm at work but don't know Norm or anything about him. Brendan told me Norm is a great guy, a good man, and he sang Norm's praises. In retrospect, it was interesting to me that Brendan mentioned Norm right away. Brendan did not say maybe I would eventually find someone, or maybe I would find someone at church. His immediate response was to consider Norm.

Today was Thanksgiving. Peter cooked the meal as always, and we had a few friends over to eat with us at noon. Peter did not eat as much as he usually ate. Everyone had left by 2:00 p.m., but we had Norm and his brother coming a little later. I asked Peter to help me with the Christmas tree, and he told me he doesn't have time because he was invited to four people's houses and was already late for the first one. It was our last Thanksgiving together as a family, and he was running off. I really thought he was seeing someone else. Brendan was incensed that Peter left to go elsewhere.

Norm and his brother, Frank, stopped by. The four of us had a great time; they stayed almost three hours! I mentioned I was supposed to go to the Grand Floridian tomorrow with some people in my training class to look at the Christmas decorations, but both bailed on me. Norm offered to go with me, so we decided to meet at the monorail as soon as he got off at 2:15 p.m. I had the day off. I wondered if he would show up.

The next day, I was waiting at the monorail station for Norm. I had butterflies in my stomach and didn't know why. This was not a date; I was not looking for it to turn into anything. It was just two people going to look at Christmas decorations, but I knew I would be extremely disappointed if Norm did not show. I saw him in the crowd, right on time, walking toward me. We took the monorail to the Grand Floridian and entered the lobby. This was my favorite Disney resort, always had been since I stayed there in 1990. The lobby was beyond beautiful with the large Christmas tree, the life-size gingerbread house, and the piano being played. It just seemed like Christmas even though it was the day after Thanksgiving. We walked around and then sat down. I told Norm I was getting a divorce. He said he was sorry. We talked about my marriage and his marriage. Talking to him was so easy. It seemed very natural. I was getting hungry and suggested we go to the Magic Kingdom for some dinner. I would pay for my own because we were not on a date. We ate at Cosmic Rays and went to Gaston's Tavern for a humongous cinnamon bun that we shared. The park was very crowded, and while walking through the crowds, Norm put his hand, very lightly, on the small of my back to guide me through. In those few seconds he was touching me, I could feel his care and concern for me. It's as if it went through me and into me. I had never had an experience like that, but it was distinct and very physical.

On our way out, we parted at the monorail station, and Norm said to me, "I'd like to do this again some time."

I responded with, "I'm game," thinking he would suggest another time to get together, but he didn't. Now I was not sure if he meant it, or if he said it to be polite. I thought about it on my way home and decided to take the bull by the horns and ask to see him again.

The next day, I texted him on our break at work and asked to have a word with him once our shift ended. He agreed and met me in the parking lot. I asked him if he meant what he said about wanting to do this again, and he said yes. I asked him if he had any plans for the rest of the day, and he did not, so I suggested we go to Epcot, and he agreed. We took the monorail over and ate at The Electric Umbrella, and again, I paid for my own meal. We did a lot of talking, and it was apparent he was interested in me. I told him I was still technically married, even though I was filing for divorce. I am an old-fashioned girl, and that meant no dating while I was still married, no touching—hand holding, hugging, kissing—and no sleeping together. If he could abide by those rules, we could hang out at the parks when our schedules allowed. Norm said he was good with those guidelines. We spent the next several hours walking around Epcot, stopping occasionally to sit and talk.

It got late, and we took the monorail back to The Magic Kingdom and then the boat over to the Polynesian Resort. Norm suggested we sit on the pier and talk for a while.

I found out Norm is three years younger than me, he lived with his ex-wife for nine years, and then was married to her for twenty-one years. He had been divorced for four years and did not date much during that time. He is a religious man. He has worked at Disney since 1980! He started out in a kitchen at one of the resorts, opened Typhoon Lagoon, drove a bus for ten years, and is now a trainer in buses. It just felt so good to be with him. Before I knew it, it was 1:00 a.m., which means I did not get home until 2:00 a.m.

When Brendan saw me the next day, he asked where I was last night and what I was doing since everything was closed when I got home. I could not believe he was checking up on me! I'm supposed to be the parent!

Norm and I didn't see each other that Sunday, but on Monday, we met at Hollywood Studios. As we were standing in line to see Kilo Ren, Norm took my left hand. I reminded him there was no touching, hand holding, etc. and asked what he was doing. He said he was getting a good look at my wedding ring so he could buy me a better one! I didn't know what to say, or if he was even serious, so I jokingly told him he better call Brendan and ask for his permission. When I got home, I told Brendan I thought Norm was going to ask

MY DARKEST DAYS, MY BRIGHTEST FUTURE

me to marry him, and if he did, I planned on saying yes. Brendan thought I had lost my mind, and I did too, but being with Norm just felt so right.

Norm called Brendan the very next day, asking his permission to marry me! Brendan was flabbergasted and didn't know what to make of any of this. He asked Norm if this wasn't going a bit too fast, so Norm asked Brendan's permission to continue seeing me, and Brendan granted it.

CHAPTER 14

Happily Ever After

OVER THE NEXT FEW WEEKS, Norm and I saw each other at the parks as our schedules allowed. He did ask me to marry him, and I said, "Yes!" When I told Brendan we were going to get married, imagine my surprise when Brendan told me he only had Norm one day of his six weeks of training. The way he spoke of Norm and sang his praises, I thought he was trained by Norm for many days. I asked Brendan how he could speak so highly of Norm after training with him for only one day, and he told me Norm is just a good man, and he knew it.

I had never done anything like this in my life. I dated Brendan's father for four years before marrying him, and Peter for two before marrying him. This was crazy, but it felt so right I had no doubts in my mind about marrying Norm.

On December 20, 2017, Peter and I were at the courthouse at 9:00 a.m. In less than ten minutes, we were granted our divorce. Once outside, Peter kissed me on the cheek and asked if I would like to go to the movies with him. He just didn't get it. I declined. After some of the recent happenings with Peter, Brendan told him he had to move out by the day of our divorce.

At 3:00 p.m., I met Norm to get our marriage license. I got a crazy notion I wanted to get married on a Disney bus and told Norm to make it happen. With as many years as he had worked for the company and all the people he knew, he should be able to pull it off. He did. Eight days later, on December 28, 2017, at 3:00 p.m., we were married on articulated bus number 5156 in the parking lot of FIW (fuel, inspect, wash—where the buses are serviced) adjacent to the training building. One of my trainers beautifully decorated the inside of the bus. A lady who worked at FIW and is also a justice of the peace married us. A few friends and coworkers attended as well as Brendan and Norm's brother, Frank. After the ceremony, the four of us went to Epcot for dinner. Norm and I spent our wedding night at the Saratoga Springs resort on the property.

I cannot believe how my life has turned out. It took me forty years to find Norm, but everything I went through during that time was worth it to end up with him. Norm never had a Disney T-shirt until he met me. I told him from the beginning I had "drank the Kool-Aid" as far as Disney was concerned. Norm says I didn't drink it; I guzzled it. But after being with Brendan and me, Norm is starting to "sip the Kool-Aid." With the three of us working in buses, we all wear the same costume, just different sizes. Being in buses brings a cohesion to our family. We know a lot of the same people and can identify with each other about our work and our experiences on the job.

Norm and Brendan are so much alike and have many of the same interests, it is hard to believe Norm is not Brendan's biological father. They enjoy one another's company, and Brendan looks up to Norm and respects him. Norm wanted children but never had any, so he is happy to have a stepson.

It wasn't until right before our wedding Norm told me he loved me from the minute he first saw me at costuming. He said not only did he think I was beautiful, but when he looked into my eyes, he saw a kindness there, but at that point, he thought he would never see me again. Once I started training in buses, Norm saw my wedding ring, and realizing I was married, thought he did not stand a chance of ever being with me.

I am immersed in Disney. I am on Disney property almost every day of my life, whether I am working, having a date night with Norm, or celebrating a special occasion in our family. We, as a family, celebrate birthdays, anniversaries, holidays, special occasions—you name it—at Disney. It never gets old. All my Christmas shopping and other gift shopping is done at one of the parks or Disney Springs. Any time we are on the property, Norm always sees someone he knows. It is like being with a celebrity. Even riding down the street, he will glance over at a Disney bus next to us and tell me he trained the person driving it. One day, I stopped by costuming in my street clothes, and a bus driver I swear I have never seen before asked me how Norm is!

CHAPTER 15

Why I wrote This Book

SEVERAL YEARS AFTER PETER WAS diagnosed as having bipolar disorder (you do not say someone is bipolar because that defines them as a person; you say they have bipolar disorder, which means they suffer from the disorder), I had the idea to write a book about living with and loving a person who had mental health issues. I truly believed his disorder was what caused him to do the things he did, and that he could not help himself. It was my intention to possibly help people who were in the same situation as I was. I felt that, while I was not an expert, I certainly had quite a bit of experience and had handled the situation relatively well.

When I married Norm, I posted the marriage on Facebook. That was probably a huge mistake on my part. I got a lot of backlash from friends and acquaintances. They all felt sorry for Peter, and some thought I had an affair and left him for Norm. That could not have been further from the truth. I know people were surprised and shocked. Peter and I had been married quite some time, and we appeared to be a very happy couple. I kept up that facade all through the years. You don't tell people your husband has a porn addiction, or that he was arrested and served time in jail.

When I posted my wedding on Facebook, I knew people would probably think I was the bad guy, but they would find out eventually Peter and I had divorced, and I had remarried, so I "ripped the BandAide off" and put it on social media. I was not going to throw Peter under the bus and call everyone and tell them the things he had done, so I became the fall guy. If I didn't want to throw Peter under the bus, why would I now write and publish a book?

While writing the bulk of this book and finishing it, my motive changed. I want to warn others who may be involved with a sociopath. I have read there is no help for a sociopath—no pill that will help/cure them, no therapy that will help/cure them. One article I came across said that if you are involved with a sociopath, don't walk away from the situation, run from it. I could not agree more.

I know we are not supposed to judge others. However, don't we all have to make judgements about the people we associate with whether they be co-workers, friends, neighbors, family members, spouses or partners and whether we want to be associated with them?

There may be people who know Peter and upon reading this book think I fabricated or exaggerated the content. I can unequivocally state that is not the case. Not too long ago, I read a fictional book titled "The Friend" by Teresa Driscoll. Teresa Driscoll was a journalist for more the twenty-five years, including fifteen years as a BBC TV news presenter. The following is quoted from the author's note at the end of her book:

"The idea for this book came from my years working as a journalist when, court case after court case, I was so often shocked by how difficult it can be to spot true 'evil' in a person.

When I started out as a reporter I imagined, naively, there would always be some sign-something in a person's behavior or background to give them away. But then I came across cases involving the kind of people who frightened me way more than the obvious misfits. The wolf in sheep's clothing. People like my fictional Emma.

The 'problem' with having a conscience is you expect other people to have one too, so you analyze and evaluate their behaviour according to your own standards. But true sociopaths have no understanding why we all worry about rules or laws...or the lives and feelings of others.

I watched so many witnesses and victims in obvious shock after coming across this kind of criminal and it was that utter *disbelief*—at being taken in—that I wanted to try and capture in this story."

Writing this book has been painful for me, revisiting things that happened during my marriage to Peter. At the time, I tried not to reflect or dwell on what he did. I tried to forgive and move on, hoping he would not repeat what he had done. That was not the case. He was a train wreck. Some things hurt me personally and deeply; others, I was just the victim of the consequences of his actions. Looking back and thinking about Peter's actions have left me mortified. Several things he did were so unconscionable/unfathomable; I chose not to include them in this book. He was not the man I thought, hoped, or wished he was. He deceived me and many others.

CHAPTER 16

Lessons Learned

I SHOULD HAVE LEFT PETER when I realized he was a pathological liar. I do not recall any one event that led me to this conclusion, but I suspected it early in our relationship. I should have left Peter when I caught him masturbating and viewing porn in our store. That was certainly a turning point in our relationship as far as any physical intimacy between us. After that day, I was no longer willing to have sex with him. It was not that I was looking to punish him or have revenge, but the thought of it disgusted me. It was certainly not the first time I had caught him viewing porn, but this time, he was masturbating with his sex toys. I should have left Peter the day he was arrested for the theft at the hospital. This was majorly worse than stealing the movie poster or stealing copper wiring from a building, but we had the store at the time, and that was probably the main reason I stayed with him. I should have left Peter when he was fired from his downtown job, not only because the official reason given was sexual harassment but because he had done something very serious, and I had no clue to what extent or what the consequences would be this time.

I finally realized each one of his run-ins with the law was more serious than the previous one. For a long time, I thought he had some sort of mental disorder, and he could not help himself, but once it dawned on me that he had no remorse for his actions, I knew our relationship was over.

Perhaps some of my motivation for staying with him was financial. I thought I could not run the store without him, but I bet I could have if push came to shove. Maybe I could have run it better without him. I thought I could not hold onto our house without his income, although with his job losses, keeping the house was never guaranteed, and wouldn't I have been better off in a different house, even an apartment, if I had some peace in my life? By the time these things started to sink in, Brendan was older, and he could have handled our breakup better than if he had been younger. Perhaps Brendan would have been better off if I had left Peter when Brendan was younger. I had no idea what Brendan saw and figured out on his own. I thought I had always hid things rather well from him, but that was not the case.

I kept thinking things would get better. I wanted things to get better. I had some major regrets in my first marriage but none in this marriage, except that I stayed in the marriage way too long. There was not one thing I could have done differently for us to stay together. I supported and loved Peter with all my heart. I lied for him and covered up for the things he did.

When I first met Peter, I did not ask him to change for me. It was his decision to stop smoking, stop drinking, and hanging out in bars. I never dreamed these changes were to worm his way into my life and my world. I thought it was wonderful he was making changes that were going to be good for him.

Even though I entertained the thought of leaving Peter more than once, I never had the unmistakable feeling I should leave him until I caught him viewing porn in Brendan's house after we moved to Florida. I knew, not long afterward, our marriage was over. After twenty years with him, I was hit with the realization he was not going to change/get better. This is who he is. I no longer wanted to be married to a man who did the things he did and would keep on doing them. I deserved better.

Peter once told me I should be glad for all the things he put me through because it made me a stronger person. I don't know I would totally agree with him, but rather than ask myself why this happened to me (I know why—it was the choices I made) and have a pity party for myself, I ask myself what I have learned.

I was in a waiting room somewhere several years ago, and the TV was on. An episode of *Dr. Phil* was being broadcast, and I never forgot it. He had a couple on his show who were about to end their marriage over a significant inheritance that they had spent in only one year. Each spouse had spent part of the money, but the other spouse did not think the expenditures were prudent. Dr. Phil asked each spouse to look back over the past year and think of what they had learned. Each had learned valuable lessons from this experience. Dr. Phil told them that a good education is not cheap, and in essence, the inheritance money they had spent was as if they had spent it on an education to learn things they could not otherwise have learned.

I think I could say the same thing about my marriage to Peter; it was a very expensive education not only with what it cost in money but what it cost me emotionally. I learned things about myself I probably could not have learned under any other circumstances. I am stronger emotionally than I ever thought I could be. I do not judge others so quickly. I have more empathy. I serve others more gladly. I have more confidence even though I made some very poor decisions along the way. I take chances that I never would have before. I try new things even if they appear to be scary. I have a love of learning and am a voracious reader. I am more positive which has had a profound impact on my life. I am more committed to my church. I developed a love for people. I have learned to trust my feelings and my instincts even if I do not know the why of a feeling or can explain it. I truly believe the feeling I had of being home, a sense of belonging, when I came to Disney on vacation all those years ago was because Norm was here at the time, and he is my soul mate. There was a connection between us, a vibe, if you will, even though we had never met. I felt that vibe when he placed his hand on the small of my back, for only a few seconds, winding our way through the crowds at the Magic Kingdom the day after Thanksgiving. I knew then that he cared about me. Not everything can be explained.

It was months after our divorce when I realized why Peter didn't want to stay married to me any longer. I could no longer help him create the image he wanted everyone to see. I always bragged about the good things Peter did, and Peter loved being in the spotlight. In

Maryland, we had a beautiful home in an upscale neighborhood, Peter's downtown job was something he was proud of, we were well known and liked in our congregation, we had many, many friends and a large network of business associations we had made during the time we had the store. I thought we had a good life, a life that most people would be happy with. Peter was content to be married to me if appearances were kept up. Once I no longer had anything to offer him by way of a nice house, lots of friends, etc., he didn't want to be with me.

After living in Florida for almost a year, it was obvious we were not going to have our own home anytime soon. Peter's job as a shift manager at the restaurant was not impressive, and we were not well known in our current congregation. I was no longer valuable to Peter to create the image he wanted the world to see.

Even though I was Peter's wife, I came to realize it was not my job to figure out what was wrong with him and try to fix it because he didn't want to. He was perfectly happy doing all the things he did if everyone saw what he wanted them to see, and I kept cleaning up and covering up the messes he made. I don't think Peter ever loved me or Brendan. He used us, and that's what sociopaths do. They use and manipulate people to get what they want, and they are extremely good at it. Peter was never sorry for the things he did; he was only sorry he got caught. Peter did all the right things for all the wrong reasons.

CHAPTER 17

Going Forward

POSTTRAUMATIC GROWTH IS WHEN TRAUMATIC experiences lead people to reframe those events and to find meaning and purpose in their lives because of the event. I feel this is the case with me and my time with Peter. I feel as though the lights have been turned on. Why is it we cannot see things until we take the time to look back and reflect? Steve Jobs once said something to the effect of, "You can only connect the dots by looking backward." We cannot see something when we are right in the middle of it. I believe that all throughout my marriage to Peter, I knew deep down inside what he was, and that our marriage was a facade, but I didn't want to believe it.

I never thought I would marry three times. I never thought I would move to Florida at age fifty-nine. I never thought I would have a dream job at Disney. I never thought I would be working the same job as Brendan. I never thought I would find the love of my life at age sixty. I never thought I would have a husband who is not only a cast member at Disney, but in my opinion, a Disney icon. I never thought I would be living fifteen minutes from Disney property. I never thought I would be on Disney property almost every day of my life.

Inside of about one year, I went from not having my own home and living with my son, to owning a home with Norm. Inside of about one year, I went from drifting from meaningless job to meaningless job to having my dream job at Disney. I am not "just a bus driver." I drive people to a place like no other where they can make memories with their family and friends that last a lifetime. Inside of about one year, I went from having no husband to having a husband who really loves me. I feel I lead a meaningful and productive life. I feel loved, safe, and secure.

I spend my days working at Disney driving a bus, decorating our home, working in my garden, and going to the parks with my family as our schedules will allow. Materialistically, I have less than I have ever had in my life, but I am happier than I have ever been in my life.

I read an article once that said that if you ask a child what they want to be when they grow up, the answer is never "loved' or "happy" or "peaceful." We put a lot of weight on success, on setting goals and reaching them. And we quantify those accomplishments. How much did you get done today? What is your salary? How big is your house? How many friends do you have on social media? Peter was my darkest days; Norm is my brightest future. I can honestly say I am loved, I am happy, and I am at peace. Norm is my "Happily Ever After." I finally found it. A true love story never ends.

THE BEGINNING.

CPSIA information can be obtained
at www.ICGtesting.com
Printed in the USA
LVHW040200210820
663761LV00008B/966

9 781645 317821